MW00807491

With Love and Gratitude for you

[signature]

ABIDING, STEADFAST JOY

Never Again Bound in a Life of Quiet Desperation

Effie Darlene Barba

By Effie Darlene Barba

~ II ~

Published in Columbia Missouri by

Effie de Barba Publishing

P.O. Box 30829

Columbia, MO 65205-3829

(407) 506-5205

© 2017 Effie Darlene Barba

Cover Artistry by Ronald Barba

"In Christ, I Am" ©2015

ALL RIGHTS RESERVED

No part of this publication may be reproduced, stored in a
retrieval system, or transmitted, in any form or by any
means, electronic, mechanical, photocopying, or otherwise—
without prior written permission.

ISBN-13: 978-0-9991193-1-0

Effie Darlene Barba

Unless otherwise noted, scripture is from the King James Version Bible

New King James Version (NKJV)
Scripture taken from the New King James Version. Copyright 1982 by
Thomas Nelson. Used by permission. All rights reserved.

The Living Bible (TLB)
The Living Bible copyright 1971 by Tyndale House Foundation. Used
by permission of Tyndale House Publishers Inc., Carol Stream, Illinois
60188. All rights reserved

Amplified Bible (AMP)
Copyright 2015 by The Lockman Foundation, La Habra, CA 90631. All
rights reserved.

New International Version (NIV)
Holy Bible, New International Version, NIV Copyright 1973, 1978,
1984, 2011 by Biblica, Inc. Used by permission. All rights reserved
worldwide.

New Living Translation (NLT)

Holy Bible, New Living Translation, copyright 1996, 2004, 2007, 2013,
2015 by Tyndale House Foundation. Used by permission of Tyndale
House Publishers Inc., Carol Stream, Illinois 60188. All rights reserved.

Abiding Steadfast Joy

Effie Darlene Barba

"The mass of men lead lives of quiet desperation. What is called resignation is confirmed desperation. From the desperate city, you go into the desperate country, and have to console yourself with the bravery of minks and muskrats. A stereotyped but unconscious despair is concealed even under what are called the games and amusements of mankind."[1]
Henry David Thoreau

Quiet Desperation lurks within the heart and soul of humanity. Hidden beneath each person's search for place, purpose and position, lies a desperate cry, afraid of being discovered unworthy. We hurry and scurry about our lives, filling every minute; afraid to be alone. Too frightened to sit quietly with our own heart's beating; because, we cannot face the despair we know lurks there within. Searching, longing to find meaning, we run from pleasure to pleasure until exhausted: only to find one's self alone in the dark of the night, once more.

Once upon a time, I found myself bound in a life of quiet desperation. Well, to be honest; more than once; perhaps more like most of my life, a quiet desperation lay just beneath the surface of my heart and mind. As a Christian, I feared telling anyone; after all, *what would they think of me or my faith?* Then, through a steady bombardment of trials, I learned three foundations of truth which lead me to a life of abiding, steadfast joy. Rising high above whatever storm I face along this journey of life, I now soar. At least most of the time, I soar. Never again to be bound in a life of quiet desperation.[1]

---

[1] Henry David Thoreau, *Walden,* (New York: Thomas Y Crowell,1910), 8

Effie Darlene Barba

TABLE OF CONTENTS

INTRODUCTION...xi

    Chapter 1 Life Amazed by Joy.............................3

FOUNDATION 1: A PLACE WITH PROMISE

    Chapter 2 Faith that Rejects the Null Hypothesis.............11

    Chapter 3: When Being and Nothingness Collide...........17

    Chapter 4 From "I Am Here" To "Who Am I?"...............23

    Chapter 5: God IS the Almighty and Sovereign LORD...29

    Chapter 6 GOD IS Perfect Righteousness and Justice.....35

    Chapter 7: God IS LOVE..41

    Chapter 8: The Great Lie...45

    Chapter 9: A Place with Promises....................................55

FOUNDATION 2: PURPOSE

    Chapter 10: Broken, Seeking Purpose.............................61

    Chapter 11: From Victims to Warriors............................67

    Chapter 12: How Can Anyone Reject Perfect Love?.......73

    Chapter 13: Out of Devastating Loss into Perfect Joy.................77

    Chapter 14: Ascending to The Edge of Glory........83

    Chapter 15: A Higher Purpose...89

    Chapter 16: 3 Foundations: Steadfast Joy.......................93

FOUNDATION 3: POSITION IN CHRIST

Chapter 17: Identity Crisis................................99

Chapter 18: I Am His Beloved.....................................107

Chapter 19: Blessed Beyond Measure 117

Chapter 20: Redeemed I Am....................................127

Chapter 21: Chosen...135

Chapter 22: Child of Almighty God............................143

Chapter 23: Heir of the Kingdom...............................155

Chapter 24: A Royal Servant.......................................165

Chapter 25: Declared a Saint, Who? Me?.....................175

Chapter 26: New Creation...189

Chapter 27: Enlightened with Clear Direction...............199

Chapter 28: Mighty Warrior..213

Chapter 29: Gifted, Endowed by God............................223

Chapter 30: United in Purpose.......................................255

Chapter 31: Therefore...In Christ I am His..............267

BECAUSE OF ALL THIS: ABIDING, STEADFAST JOY

Chapter 32: Knowing These Foundational Truths; Now What?..279

POEMS

Out of the Nothingness..52

As God's Beloved...115

In Christ, I am God's own Beloved...........................132

With God as My Father; Yes, I Would....................152

An Act of Grace...210

Gifts of the Spirit..252

A Talk with God...283

BIBLIOGRAPHY

BIBLIOGRAPHY..287

Effie Darlene Barba

INTRODUCTION

The gunshots rang out in the middle of the night. My hand froze on the doorknob, for a second, until I heard Pete's cousin screaming. A moment before, I had leapt from my bed to rush out into the living room when I heard Pete say, "I need a witness for this"; but before I could open the door, I heard the gunshot blast through the dark. Frozen, my hand clutched the doorknob motionless.

I heard the cousin screaming for help. Pushing back the fear, I flung open the door and rushed into the living room. Immediately, I saw Pete's limp body slumped in the recliner. The gun lay in his lap with his hand loosely about the handle and his finger motionless on the trigger. Blood was dripping from his mouth. His breath was shallow as I gently reclined the chair, tipping his head back so he could breathe.

So many years, I had prayed for my beloved husband. This was not the answer I had longed and pleaded for. I wanted to scream or cry; but, I had to get help. I had to comfort my son whom I heard screaming desperately from the other bedroom, awakened by the blast of the gun. Going through the motions, I called for help between running back and forth to the bedroom to check on my son. I wanted to pray that all would be ok. However, deep in my heart I knew, it was too late.

It would be a month or more before I could ask the question my aching heart wanted to ask. "How do you keep trusting God, when you don't understand?"

Through so many years, I had watched this man battle with a bipolar disorder. Such a brilliant mind, a genius; yet, he was plagued by moments of grandeur followed by utter despair. There were moments in which his battle spilled over into violence toward me. The bruises and scars on my body were little to compare to those in my heart. Yet, I knew that it had been God's Grace abiding within me that allowed me to forgive the moments of violence that resulted from Pete's internal battle; because, I knew the power to love unconditionally was more than I was capable of. After all, God had prepared me through my own mother's bipolar disorder to see past the sometimes-violent exterior.

Deep, hidden under the harsh exterior, I saw the heart of this man. His heart was kind, gentle and loving; although, often masked by his own fears of love. Because he had been so hurt, injured as a child; he was broken. But, if truth be told; aren't we all broken in some way.

I did know this one thing, from the day, we first met. I loved him with a love greater than this human heart was capable of. I realize now, that kind of love only came from God Himself; because, God had a perfect plan of love for me and for Pete amid all the brokenness, pain and despair. Though I could not see it at first, I see it clearly now.

TRUSTING GOD WHEN YOU DON'T UNDERSTAND THE ANSWER

For years, I had prayed that God would heal Pete. The first step I knew must be his finding Christ as his Savior. All the years of sorrow and disappointment in his past had lead Pete to not believe in God. He was well versed in science, history, arts, and philosophy; none of which could comfort his soul. Over time, God demonstrated through me a steadfast devotion and love toward Pete. God gave me a heart of forgiveness and strength; until, one-day Pete began to want what I had.

Although, I must confess that through those years, my faith struggled at times. I often felt defeated. Often I had told God, "I am done. I cannot do this." Each time, I thought I could not go another step, God filled my heart with compassion, love and understanding. Then, miraculously I would take another step, followed by another; until I was moving ahead, forward again. Pete saw God's strength and grace, peaking out of my actions; despite, my not seeing it in myself. When I thought, I was weak, failing; God shone through me as strong and gracious. I do not fully know how; but, I do know that must have been the case.

As God drew Pete toward Himself, I watched as this former atheist began to desire God's word and His truth. For me, I rejoiced in that hope. God would heal him! I knew it! And then, all would be well.

But alas, God's answer came and certainly, was not what I had believed it would be. My heart broke into a thousand pieces that day. Each piece laying shattered before me.

Pete had accepted Jesus Christ as his Savior six months prior to his death; then, instead of a miraculous healing here on earth, God chose to allow this. Yes, because he was saved; he is in heaven, healed. Not the healing I had desired; but, the healing God chose. God's plan may not have been the one I thought best; however, God is always good and knew what was the best plan. All the years of my life have lead me to see the wonder of God's Grace and love toward Pete and toward me. Pete's death was 23 years ago; although, I remember my pain as though it were yesterday; although, now the memories are like a cool spring breeze after a long winter.

~ xiii~

A STEP TOWARD FAITH AND STEADFAST JOY

Every step of this journey; God has been my hope, my strength, and the guiding light leading me to realize, God is my Abiding, Steadfast Joy. In Christ, I have found peace, hope, faith, and joy. Yes, true steadfast, unchanging Joy abiding evermore within my heart.

The tragic death of my husband had not been the only trial that I faced; although, perhaps it stands out as a turning point in how I viewed trials. There were many more trials yet to come. During the years following Pete's death, I faced cancer, illness, financial setbacks and multiple surgeries. I felt my heart break many times when I watched my children struggle, facing their own challenges. Yet, during all that I have walked through; God has been there gently drawing me closer to His side. In the darkest moments, He shone forth His light to guide my way. He has proven that He is my JOY, my love, and my greatest treasure.

What God did through allowing all the sorrows, setbacks, and even failures of my own making; was to transform my regenerate heart and to change my thinking pattern. Over the years of trials, sufferings, and tragedies, He was at work using each one to teach me the three foundational truths of everlasting Joy in Him. Step by step, He has shown forth His Glory, Majesty and Sovereignty in my life. His Grace, His love has changed how I view the storms of this life. He changed my mind's view of yesterday, today and tomorrow.

TRUSTING GOD WITH MY LIFE AND MY CHILDREN

This not only transformed how I viewed my life. It transformed how I see God's mighty hand in the lives of my children, my friends and the world in which we live.

My sons were mere teenagers when their father committed suicide. They too, had to face many trials; but, God was with us. I cried with each of their trials; but, I came to trust that God would Sovereignly guide their life as well. Oh, yes; as I mother, I wanted them spared from the trials. They had already lived through so much because I chose to stay with Pete; obeying, the promptings I now am certain were ordained by God. During those years, I held tight to the whispering promise God gave to me each time I protested, "What about my children? I must protect them. " Then, God whispered, "I have bid you to stay and I will protect them. You will see one day all that I will accomplish in their lives."

Still, when I pause and consider the truth. My trials were what brought me to this intimate place with God, where the storms cannot destroy my hope and joy in Him. If God had used all the trials in my life to lead me to a place of steadfast joy, hope and faith; then, would He not do the same with my children? So, each trial they faced; I prayed that God would reveal Himself to them. Thank God, they all do profess a saving knowledge of Christ. So, as a mother; I let go and trust God to finish all that He has planned in their life, His way.

Psalm 61:1-5,8

Hear my cry, O God; attend unto my prayer.
From the end of the earth will I cry unto thee,

when my heart is overwhelmed: lead me to the rock that is higher than I. For thou hast been a shelter for me, and a strong tower from the enemy. I will abide in thy tabernacle forever: I will trust in the covert of thy wings. Selah. For thou, O God, hast heard my vows: thou hast given me the heritage of those that fear thy name. So, will I sing praise unto thy name for ever, that I may daily perform my vows.

AMAZED BY JOY

Through many tumultuous trials, I have found hope, joy, and faith; because, God has been at work to teach me the truth. During the raging storms of life, I have learned that there are three foundational truths which serve as an anchor to our spirit and souls. I want to share with you these three foundational truths, so, you might awaken each morning amazed by joy in your life.

I have found, that God is the rock higher than I; whenever, my heart is overwhelmed. He is my shelter and my strong tower from the enemy. I will trust in the covert of His wings where I will sing His praise every day. He has amazed me with His Grace and He has amazed me with His Joy throughout this journey. Trusting God is the only way to find joy, hope, and peace in this life and all of eternity as well. We do not have to live lives of quiet desperation. Come along this journey and let me share with you three truths: the foundation on which you may stand whatever you may face today.

Effie Darlene Barba

Dedication

I dedicate this book to God who has been my steadfast, abiding joy. He loved me unconditionally, through it all. And to His son, who paid the price for my salvation.

Effie Darlene Barba

Chapter 1:
Life Amazed by Joy

No one could be more Amazed by Joy, than I; because, this journey called life is filled with many trials, sorrows, and storms. At least, mine was; and I suspect, your reality includes moments which push you to the edge of despair, as well. Yet, out of those struggles, God amazed me with the truth of His magnificent Grace, Love and Glory. Through the trials, He taught me to trust Him with every detail of my life. Furthermore, He, step by step, transformed my thinking process so I could see circumstances through His eyes, rather than, through the finiteness of my own eyes. My heart and thoughts could never face life undaunted by the storms; until, He changed my heart and my thoughts from the inside out.

Storms are an inevitable part of this journey on earth; yet, God has a plan for our good, to all those who seek Him. All who know Jesus Christ as Savior and Lord are assured that God is working everything together for their good. He wants us to live with hope, joy, love and peace within our hearts; as, He shares with us His Glory. He wants us to live every moment of life Amazed by Joy-His Joy in us- steadfast and abiding deep within our spirits. This begins by learning these three foundational truths!

Knowing the truth about our place in this Universe, our purpose and our position in Christ is paramount to discovering a life filled with hope, energy, and abounding joy. Once we know these truths, we think about and view every circumstance differently than we would have otherwise. So, yes! How we think is very important; however, our thoughts must be founded upon the truth of God's word.

Don't get me wrong, I am not saying no trials will come or that you will get all your eyes desire by thinking a different way. What I am saying: knowing these 3 foundational truths, your heart remains filled with joy; even when, your world is turned upside down.

> *Listen carefully. Keep these thoughts ever in mind; let them penetrate deep within your heart, for they will mean real life for you and radiant health (Proverbs 4:20-22 TLB).*

THREE TRUTHS YOU MUST KNOW

1. **My place in this Universe including God's promise**

   Unless I truly know my place in this vast universe and His promise to me through faith; there is no hope; because, my relationship with my Creator begins with knowing this.

   > *faith is the substance of things hoped for, the evidence of things not seen. Through faith we understand that the worlds were framed by the word of God, so that things which are seen were not made of things which do appear. ...for he that cometh to God must believe that he is, and that he is a rewarder of them that diligently seek him (Hebrews 11:1,3,6).*

The foundation of faith: Knowing God IS and that He is the rewarder of them that diligently seek Him. This is key #1. God IS the creator, the Lord, the Sovereign Ruler of heaven and earth. He is All Glory, Perfect Righteousness; as well as, Justice. Beyond that He is perfect Love, rich with mercy and Grace. When I really know this as true; I recognize that I am not master of my own destiny. My place is not the center of the universe.

I was created by an Almighty God. My life is in His hands to do with as He pleases; yet, there is this promise. "He is a rewarder of those who diligently seek Him." Faith, hope and joy are found in His presence. I must first know this truth, if I hope to find true and lasting joy along this journey.

2. **The Purpose for Which I was Created**

Secondly, I must understand the purpose for which I was created. Most of my life, I heard people say, "I am created to bring God Glory." Sounds good perhaps; yet, the longer I lived this Christian life, the more I realized: there is nothing innately inside of me that could add to or bring God Glory. If I did anything right, good or glorious; it was Him working through me and not anything my own guilty hands could perform for Him. So, I needed to know the purpose for which I was created.

Then, one day I read John 17. That was the prayer Jesus prayed as He walked toward the Garden of Gethsemane. In that prayer, Jesus candidly proclaimed the purpose of creation; and, the purpose for each who would come to accept Him as Savior. Reading that prayer, that day; I learned that God created me so that He might shower upon me His love, fill me with His Joy, and share with me His Glory. His most glorious act is the salvation of one soul. When, He chooses to use me in that, by using my testimony; He has shared with me a small piece of His Glory. Certainly, He doesn't need me to help in the salvation of another; but, sometimes, He uses me anyway. That is Grace Magnified!

3. **My Position in Christ**

Thirdly, we, the followers of Christ, must know our position in Him. Ephesians chapters 1-3 meticulously details our position in Christ. There I learned that in Christ, I am God's chosen, redeemed, beloved, gifted, enlightened Child; heir of the Kingdom of God, servant by choice, a new creation and declared a saint. None of this, because of my own merit; but, by the blood shed by Christ for me. In Christ, I possess everything I could ever need. Knowing this, releases me from the chains of sin, sorrow and despair.

When Knowledge Transforms our Thoughts and our Hearts

Knowing these three foundational truths transforms not only how we think toward God; it also prepares our heart to fully experience a relationship with God. He becomes more precious with each day we live. Then, as our eyes become more focused on Him; the circumstances of this life grow dim in comparison to His Majesty. We begin to see life's circumstances through His eyes. Therein, we find that each day; no matter what storms come, we are Amazed by Joy: His Steadfast, Abiding Joy in us.

Therefore, this book I've written for you; so, you too, can live a life overflowing with steadfast joy, hope, and love: undaunted by the storms of this world. My greatest desire is that you experience steadfast, abiding joy; never again, to be trapped in quiet desperation.

Let me leave you today with this verse:

> *Finally, brethren, whatever things are true, whatever things are noble, whatever things are just, whatever things are pure, whatever things are lovely, whatever things are of good report, if there is any virtue and if there is anything praiseworthy— meditate on these things. Philippians 4:8 (NKJV)*

Effie Darlene Barba

FOUNDATION #1
PLACE WITH PROMISE

Effie Darlene Barba

Chapter 2:

Faith That Rejects the Null Hypothesis of Life

It was June 1995. I was uncertain as to what the future might bring. My world had collapsed with Pete's death, or so it seemed. For so many years, my world wrapped around loving and caring for Pedro Barba Arroyo. Willingly, I watched as all our resources dwindled; pouring everything into helping him get well. We had lost a thriving medical practice, lost our home in Texas, and moved to Mexico; all because of one hope: Pete would get well. He died on July 23, 1994.

Then, I spent nearly a year traveling between Pachuca, Hgo, Mexico and my hometown of Dexter, Mo. All that had been left of what appeared to the world's eyes as a prosperous life; now, was some land in Mexico which Pete had left the children. Once their land had been secured, I made the final trip from Pachuca to Dexter by way of the "carreterra" (Mexican highways).

No other choice lay before me; except, to pick up the pieces of my life and start again, for the sake of my children. I would need to find the faith to reject the Null Hypothesis of my own life.

My grief was overwhelming still. My hopes dashed. I believed with all my heart, God would heal Pete here on this earth. Yet, God chose not to. Instead, God chose to take Him home.

Pete had accepted Christ as His Savior only a few short months before his death. I did not question God's Sovereign choice; yet, I also knew there was a lot of brokenness left behind in me and in my children. Unimaginable scars and gaping wounds that needed to heal.

Then I did what some would believe utter foolishness. After arriving in Dexter to start this new life, I had looked for a job. When I did not find one; and after much prayer, I decided to pack up my children and go on an adventure in Disney World.

IGNORING THE COST

I flew Melissa in from California, invited my nephew Derek, loaded up my van, and all of us, went on a trip to Florida. I ignored the cost as I spent what I had on Disney World parks, Hard Rock Café, and Universal Studios. We stood on the beach at Daytona; and then, we returned home. I wanted to restore hope and joy into the hearts of my family. I was uncertain of what life would bring tomorrow; but, I did know that whatever it brought: God was at my side and would be, through it all. Oh, by the way, as soon as I returned I had a job waiting for me. That vacation had been a leap of faith for me and a trip for all of us to remember.

Which brings me to the first foundational truth necessary in this life! In Hebrews 11 we are given a definition of faith as:

> Now faith is the substance of things hoped for, the evidence of things not seen... he that cometh to God must believe that he is, and that he is a rewarder of them that diligently seek him. Hebrews 11:1,6

Faith begins at this very point: Knowing that God IS and that He rewards those who diligently seek Him.

GOD IS

God is Sovereign Lord, Creator of the Universe, the Great I AM. Faith begins with knowing this as true! Without seeing God as Almighty Supreme Ruler of this Universe; there cannot be any faith. We must know in the core of our hearts that He is Glorious, Righteous, and Just in all that He does. Once we recognize who He is, we can see our place in this Universe as His created beings; over whom, He reigns supreme.

Furthermore, we can then believe fully His promise when He says He rewards those who diligently seek Him. With open arms of love, He reaches forth to provide for, protect, and draw all men to Himself; despite His knowing many will reject His offer. Relentlessly, He reaches forth to demonstrate His power and His might; but, alas only a few will come. Still, for those who do His promises ring true.

THE POWER TO REJECT THE NULL HYPOTHESIS

Where is the power that can give a weary, broken soul hope? Can it be found in the recesses of a despairing soul, by merely proclaiming that all is well? When everything is lost, where does one find the strength to stand again?

In statistics, we learn: Power is the strength to reject the null hypothesis! The null hypothesis believes everything is by chance only. If my life is by chance only, then I have no power to reject the null hypothesis. Indeed, I am powerless to face the storms of this life. If the null hypothesis were true for my life, then I could never stand firm with hope or joy. Instead of hope, life would be despairingly hopeless.

But, I have hope; because this I KNOW-*all things work together for good, for those who know Christ, for those who are called according to His purpose* (Romans 8:28).

The Power to reject the null hypothesis for my life is secured by the death and the resurrection of Jesus Christ. No other religion, philosophy, nor thought process contains the power to sustain hope during life's tragic moments of utter despair. This is the message that Paul, Peter, James, John and all the early believers were willing to suffer and die for. They had seen the risen Christ; and they knew, that in Him, we have newness of life.

Through the entirety of my life, God's hand of love never let go of this flailing heart. He remained ever present; when I believed and when I doubted His love, he stood steadfast in His love for me. From the moment, I first asked Jesus to come into my heart, He has never let go of me. That is why, I can declare without a doubt that Jesus Christ and the gospel message IS the Power to Reject the Null hypothesis of your life as well.

ACTS 17: 24-31

God that made the world and all things therein, seeing that he is Lord of heaven and earth, dwelleth not in temples made with hands; Neither is worshipped with men's hands, as though he needed anything, seeing he giveth to all life, and breath, and all things; And hath made of one blood all nations of men for to dwell on all the face of the earth, and hath determined the times before appointed, and the bounds of their habitation; That they should seek the Lord, if haply they might feel after him, and find him, though he be not far from every one of us: For in him we live, and move, and have our being; as certain also of your own poets have said, For we are also his offspring. Forasmuch then as we are the offspring of God, we ought not to think that the Godhead is like unto gold, or silver, or stone, graven by art and man's device. And the times of this ignorance God winked at; but now comma (Sartre and Barnes, Being and Nothingness 1969)*ndeth all men everywhere to repent: Because he hath appointed a day, in the which he will judge the world in righteousness by that man (Jesus) whom he hath ordained; whereof he hath given assurance unto all men, in that he hath raised him from the dead."*

GOD REIGNS SUPREME

As for me, I am glad that I did not know all the trials that still lay before me when I chose to take that vacation. Nor do I know what storms yet lay before me. Unexpected storms blow into our lives without warning. Yet, even when I am laden with moments of great heartbreak; this I KNOW!

God is in control and He has a plan for my good and that my life will be prosperous. Oh, perhaps not the prosperous that the world considers. Still, I know it will be prosperous in Joy unspeakable found in Christ, hope that is never dying, and an ever-flowing fountain of love within my heart. GOD IS the power to reject the null hypothesis of life-yours or mine.

Our life does not happen by chance. God guides, ordains, and sovereignly remains in control. His plan commands good to all those who seek Him. Furthermore, all who seek Him will find Him. That is Good News!

Chapter 3:

When Being and Nothingness Collide

Faith begins by knowing God IS (Hebrews 11:6). Is (the second first participle of the word be), a very simple word with profound meaning. "God IS" proclaims the truth of God's name as "I AM": the very essence of BEING. This goes far beyond just existing; rather, it is the state of being without which nothing can be or exist.

The essence of everything begins with God who IS the creator, controller, majestic ruler of the Universe. Outside of His Being, there is nothingness. With that truth, I realize I am nothing until I am found in Him who breaths into me, life. He who created me, formed me in my mother's womb: knew me before He created the earth. Think about that. My very existence is because of His Being the Great I AM.

Our vain hearts yearn to be. We want purpose, meaning, and reason for our life. Yet in our nothingness, we have none; until being and nothingness collide into one.

God IS light. Therefore, outside of His light there is utter darkness. I could not exist were it not for God's will for me to exist. I, one person among all the people of this earth; reside on a small area of this earth, a mere speck orbiting a distant corner of the Milky Way Galaxy, which as a galaxy is miniscule compared to all the other galaxies in this universe.

So, who are we? How can I find any being in my miniscule existence apart from God's Grace; who despite my nothingness, loves me with an everlasting love? "*For in him we live, and move, and have our being*" (Acts 17:28).

BEING AND NOTHINGNESS

Jean Paul Sartre, a famous atheistic philosopher, portrayed the depth of despair that plagues humanity both in his book "*Being and Nothingness*", as well as his novel, "nausea". Let's look at a few of those quotes:

"I want to leave, to go somewhere where I should be really in my place, where I would fit in . . . but my place is nowhere; I am unwanted." [2]

"My thought is me: that's why I can't stop. I exist because I think... and I can't stop myself from thinking. At this very moment - it's frightful - if I exist, it is because I am horrified at existing. I am the one who pulls myself from the nothingness to which I aspire [3]

"Nothingness lies coiled in the heart of being - like a worm [4]

"I exist, that is all, and I find it nauseating." [5]

What depth of despair exists, when one tries to become by one's own endeavors to be. I cannot find being out

[2] Jean Paul Sartre, *Nausea,* trans. Lloyd Alexander, (New York: New Directions, 1964),
[3] Ibid.,100
[4] Jean Paul Sartre, *Being and Nothingness,* Barnes, H. (Trans.) (New York: Washington Square Press, 1969),56
[5] Ibid.

of nothingness unless true Being penetrates my nothingness. Without my knowing God IS everything; I cannot discover anything of meaning within this world.

TRANSFORMING FINITE INTO INFINITE-AN ACT OF GRACE

I am hopeless to overcome any obstacle before me; were it not for God's gracious hand of love reaching for me. In my nothingness, Infinite love, grace, strength has entered to proclaim me as His own. He, who causes light to shine upon the just and the unjust, chose me to be His child.

I cannot understand the magnitude of this until I recognize the utter futility of my own doing and being in this world. God NEEDS nothing from me; yet, He wants a personal relationship with me and desires to fulfill all my needs. Stop, and think about that for just a moment!

My view of every circumstance that enters my life transforms when I acknowledge my nothingness and His Being. When He enters my nothingness, then my being exists because of His Being. His essence becomes my essence.

Ponder this truth:

He is perfect righteousness, justice, glory, love, and might. He is the light of the world who chose to pay the penalty for my sin; that I might have eternal life in His presence. The beauty of that life begins here upon this earth, where I can trust Him with every detail of my life. It then extends into eternity where one day, I will behold Him in all His Glory.

GOD'S GRACIOUS WORDS

I am crucified with Christ: nevertheless, I live; yet not I, but Christ liveth in me: and the life which I now live in the flesh I live by the faith of the Son of God, who loved me, and gave himself for me (Galatians 2:20).

But God, who is rich in mercy, for his great love wherewith he loved us, Even when we were dead in sins, hath quickened us together with Christ, (by grace ye are saved;)And hath raised us up together, and made us sit together in heavenly places in Christ Jesus: That in the ages to come he might shew the exceeding riches of his grace in his kindness toward us through Christ Jesus (Ephesians 2:5-7).

For we are his workmanship, created in Christ Jesus unto good works, which God hath before ordained that we should walk in them (Ephesians 2:10).

CONCLUDING THOUGHTS

Only one hope stands in the corridors of life capable of transforming my nothingness into being: God! That can only happen when being and nothingness collide into one.

That is, when God's Spirit collides with our spirit to become one through faith in Jesus Christ. He is our hope. We need first to recognize our nothingness that we might find being in Him.

CONCLUDING THOUGHT BITES

When Being and Nothingness Collide, I become one in Christ by faith, through grace. My nothingness can only become being by accepting Salvation's Gift from Yahweh (the Great I AM).

Effie Darlene Barba

CHAPTER 4:

FROM "I AM HERE" TO "WHO AM I?"

Moses, by all human accounts; looked like the most unlikely person to lead the nation of Israel. Certainly, his life was spared; when his mother hid him in a basket by the river so that Pharaoh's daughter would find him and raise him in the palace. But, he had long ago run in fear from Egypt, after having stood up against a guard who had beaten one of the Israeli slaves. In the quiet life that he had become accustomed to as a shepherd, he had no thought of returning to Egypt. Then, God called upon Moses to lead the people to the promised land.

Indeed, Exodus 3 marks the first-time God refers to Himself as I AM. For you and I to embrace the truth that God IS, we must understand the truth of God's own name for Himself as I AM. God IS the Absolute Being, the eternal creator of heaven and earth.

God is transcendent; meaning He exists independent of the materiality of this world; while at the same time, He is immanently involved in every detail of this, His creation. To begin to understand the absoluteness of God, we must begin to see Him as Yahweh. To do so, let's take a moment to look at the conversation between Moses and God; wherein God first refers to Himself as YAHWEH (I AM).

A pivotal moment for Moses occurred here, as he came to discover his place in God's Story. We too, can find our place in the universe by understanding God's own name for himself as I AM.

ONE MAN'S PERSONAL ENCOUNTER WITH GOD

So, it was that day; Moses was out tending to his sheep, peacefully minding his own business; when he saw a burning bush. Despite it burning, it wasn't consumed by the fire, which was quite an oddity. Because Moses wondered about this rarity, he approached. As he approached, he heard a voice cry out, "Moses." To this he replied, "here am I".

"Draw not nigh hither: put off thy shoes from off thy feet, for the place whereon thou standest is holy ground. Moreover, he said, I am the God of thy father, the God of Abraham, the God of Isaac, and the God of Jacob. And Moses hid his face; for he was afraid to look upon God. And the LORD said, I have surely seen the affliction of my people which are in Egypt, and have heard their cry by reason of their taskmasters; for I know their sorrows;

And I am come down to deliver them out of the hand of the Egyptians, and to bring them up out of that land unto a good land and a large, unto a land flowing with milk and honey; unto the place of the Canaanites, and the Hittites, and the Amorites, and the Perizzites, and the Hivites, and the Jebusites. Now therefore, behold, the cry of the children of Israel is come unto me: and I have also seen the oppression wherewith the Egyptians oppress them (Exodus 3: 6-9).

God demonstrated clearly His personal knowledge of the affairs of the world and His definite plan. Not idly watching the events with no plan, God knew everything about this encounter before Moses had ever been born.

GOD IS THE ABSOLUTE BEING

Having obtained the full attention of Moses, God declares His plan,

> *Come now therefore, and I will send thee unto Pharaoh, that thou mayest bring forth my people the children of Israel out of Egypt. And Moses said unto God, Who am I, that I should go unto Pharaoh, and that I should bring forth the children of Israel out of Egypt?* (Exodus 3: 10-11).

Did you notice that? Moses, who previously answered "Here I am!" now responds "Who am I?" Don't miss this! When God declares His Being, Moses recognizes his own nothingness and his powerlessness to be anything apart from God.

Moses then begins a long dissertation with God concerning all the reasons he cannot be the one to perform this task. To which, God essentially says; "I know that; but I AM is with you. I am the voice you need, the strength and the courage you don't have. Moses, still arguing said, "No one would believe me." To which God replies,

> *I AM THAT I AM: and he said, Thus shalt thou say unto the children of Israel, I AM hath sent me unto you. And God said moreover unto Moses, Thus shalt thou say unto the children of Israel, the LORD God of your fathers, the God of Abraham, the God of Isaac, and the God of Jacob, hath sent me unto you: this is my name for ever, and this is my memorial unto all generations* (Exodus 3:14-15).

God declared His Name forever to be I AM. Furthermore, God proclaimed this truth, "Without me there is none other." No being exists apart from God willing their existence; because, God is the absolute being

GOD IN HIS ABSOLUTE BEING OF GRACE

There is no task too great for God, the absolute being; who in Sovereignty reigns over this world. His Grace and Mercy, patiently abides; awaiting the Salvation of one more soul before He reigns down His final just and righteous judgement upon this earth. He has given His Only Begotten Son and extended forth His greatest gift of salvation through Jesus Christ.

And now He holds steady His final hand of judgement against all those who choose to spit upon this His offer of Mercy and Grace. He endures the injustice of all those who declare their own significance apart from God; never, recognizing their insignificant, finite unimportance in the Universe, denying the very God who gave them life. Despite their rebellion, He allows them to enjoy the beauty of His creation.

God will complete and perform all that He has planned on the earth. He is calling to you from the burning bushes of trials in this life; to come, remove your shoes and step on Holy Ground before Him. He asks that you, too; change your stance before Him from "Here I am" to "Who am I?" Only then, can you truly find your place in this Universe; as you find your being in God-the Absolute Being.

Effie Darlene Barba

Chapter 5:

God IS THE Almighty and Sovereign LORD

Over the previous three chapters, I wrote to you about the first foundational truth needed to awaken each morning amazed by a steadfast, abiding joy in your heart, undaunted by the storms of life; to never again, live bound by a life of quiet desperation.

That Foundation of truth: Faith begins with knowing God IS. Within those two words we begin to see the characteristics of God as the Great I AM.

We are nothingness, having no being; until we find our Being in Him, who created each of us and gave us life. Beyond knowing our existence in Him, we need also to understand that God IS Almighty! His power and might is above all other powers. He rules with Sovereign might over the affairs of men, women, and children; just as, He rules over the stars, the animal kingdom, and everything within the Universe. When we know Him as the Almighty Ruler; then, we must conclude that He will accomplish His purpose in our life. He cannot and will not fail; because, He is Almighty God, Sovereign ruler of the Universe.

Even in those moments that we do not understand the plan; we can trust the heart of Almighty God, who loved us with all His might. Nothing happens in my life or yours; but, that God Almighty has allowed or ordained it to happen to fulfill His purpose in our lives.

He, who created me, knows every crevice of my heart. Furthermore, He knows exactly what is needed to transform my heart into one that finds my joy, my hope, and my pleasure in Him. Ultimately, He knows that, in the end; my heart can only find its true satisfaction in a personal relationship with Him. In other words, He IS the only one who can fulfill all the desires of my heart: He IS everything my heart desires.

ISAIAH 46:9-10,12-13 (NKJV)

> *Remember the former things of old, For I am God, and there is no other; I am God, and there is none like Me,*
> *Declaring the end from the beginning, And from ancient times things that are not yet done,*
> *Saying, 'My counsel shall stand, And I will do all My pleasure, ... Indeed, I have spoken it; I will also bring it to pass. I have purposed it; I will also do it. "Listen to Me, you stubborn-hearted, who are far from righteousness: I bring My righteousness near, it shall not be far off; My salvation shall not linger.*

God pleads with mankind to draw near to him. Furthermore, He draws near to us. This he does despite our pushing away, ignoring His call. We, so stubbornly, desire our own way; believing, we really know what is best for our own lives. We think we know what will bring us pleasure; only to be disappointed repeatedly with counterfeit joys. In His Sovereignty, often God allows us to face disappointment, trials and sorrows; so that we might ultimately seek Him; and then, find our rest and comfort in Him. When we begin to see our trials through His Almighty Hands of love, we learn to seek Him in the center of every storm. His only desire, in the end, is for our fulfillment of Joy, Love, and Glory in Him; because, He IS all that we need.

AN EXAMPLE WITH JOB

Job had been a righteous man, even before the disaster came. He prayed, offered sacrifice, and worshipped God; however, he never fully understood God's almighty power to bring him into a closer fellowship with God, until Job lost everything.

He knew of God before the tragedy; but, he knew God intimately, after the tragedy struck. I won't try to recall the entire story of Job here; but, I urge you to go to the book of Job and read it for yourself. I do want to point out this one statement by one of Job's "friends" and refer you to God's own dissertation that followed in Job 38-42, in which God declares once more, Himself as the Almighty Ruler over all.

"You who think you know so much, teach the rest of us how we should approach God. For we are too dull to know! With your wisdom, would we then dare to approach him? Well, does a man wish to be swallowed alive? For as we cannot look at the sun for its

~ 31~

brightness when the winds have cleared away the clouds, neither can we gaze at the terrible majesty of God breaking forth upon us from heaven, clothed in dazzling splendor. We cannot imagine the power of the Almighty, and yet he is so just and merciful that he does not destroy us. No wonder men everywhere fear him! For he is not impressed by the world's wisest men!"
Job 37 (TLB)

HOW TO APPROACH GOD ALMIGHTY

The dissertation of Job's friend, at first; sounds true. Only, the friend is missing one thing! We are called upon by God to approach His throne of Grace, boldly. He bids us to commune with Him. Yes, we should fear Him; if we do not allow Him into our own lives. Yet, if I come to Him with a heart humbled by the reality that He is Sovereign Lord; and I, a sinner in need of Him to provide for me His Righteousness: He will save me. Then, He will do the work needed to transform my heart. He will take responsibility for it all; if only, I humbly come to Him, desiring to enter covenant with Him. Then, understanding all this; let us approach God, desiring His covenant. Knowing we cannot fulfill our part of the covenant, were it not for grace.

That thou shouldest enter into covenant with the LORD thy God, and into his oath, which the LORD thy God maketh with thee this day: That he may establish thee today for a people unto himself, and that he may be unto thee a God

And the LORD thy God will circumcise thine heart, and the heart of thy seed, to love the LORD thy God with all thine heart, and with all thy soul, that thou mayest live. And the LORD thy God will make thee plenteous in every work of thine hand, for the LORD will again rejoice over thee for good. If thou shalt hearken unto the voice of the LORD thy God, to keep his commandments and his statutes which are written in this book of the law, and if thou turn unto the LORD thy God with all thine heart, and with all thy soul (Deuteronomy 29: 12-13 and 30:6,9).

A CALL TO APPROACH THE ALMIGHTY

When we fully understand that God is Almighty, we may at first tremble; however, He has provided a way for our salvation through Jesus Christ, who was the propitiation for our sins.

For we have not an high priest which cannot be touched with the feeling of our infirmities;

> *but was in all points tempted like as we are, yet*
> *without sin. Let us therefore come boldly unto*
> *the throne of grace, that we may obtain mercy,*
> *and find grace to help in time of need*
> (Hebrews 4:15-16).

We can trust God Almighty to complete His Purpose and plan in our lives. No matter what comes or confronts us; we can trust that He has the best plan for our lives.

> *we know that all things work together for good*
> *to them that love God, to them who are the*
> *called according to his purpose* (Romans
> 8:28).

Chapter 6

GOD IS Perfect Righteousness and Justice

He is the Rock, his work is perfect: for all his ways are judgment: A God of truth and without iniquity, just and right is he (Deuteronomy 32:4).

Do you truly know in your heart of hearts that this is true? All too often, we question God's integrity. Particularly doubt arises when we see tragedies occur in the world, or in our own lives. We may, in those moments, stutter out some phrase of trusting God's intentions. Meanwhile, deep within our hearts; we wonder how a God of perfect righteousness and justice allows tragedies to continue upon this earth we live. However, if we truly understand the perfect righteousness and justice of God; instead, we would marvel at His amazing Grace suspending His declaration of final judgement on this earth and all of humanity.

There is no greater portrait of God's Glory than found in this characteristic of His nature intertwined within all His characteristics of Glory. Certainly, His Perfect Righteousness and Justice must be every bit as great a part of His being as is His Sovereignty and His Loving Grace. There cannot truly exist Grace; were there not justice, as well. Think about this. Can I be forgiven my sins, were I not first condemned?

As Romans 3: 23 tells us clearly, *"All have sinned, and come short of the glory of God"*

Until I truly know God IS Perfect Righteousness and Justice; I cannot fully appreciate my predicament, nor can I embrace the truth of His gift of Grace, purchased at such a tremendous price. Neither can I understand the price He paid for my salvation.

ROMANS 3:24-26

> *Being justified freely by his grace through the redemption that is in Christ Jesus: Whom God hath set forth to be a propitiation through faith in his blood, to declare his righteousness for the remission of sins that are past, through the forbearance of God; To declare, I say, at this time his righteousness: that he might be just, and the justifier of him which believeth in Jesus.*

Jesus Christ bore the penalty of our sin. Only because of Christ's sacrifice, I am declared righteous before an Almighty God. God is Just in all that He does; yet, He justified me through His Own Son's sacrifice.

He cannot deny His perfect righteousness nor Justice! Therefore, He provided the way for sinners to be saved. When I fully grasp the truth of His Perfect Righteousness and Justice; then, I can no longer question anything that He allows. For by all rights, He could have spoken, in a moments time, and destroyed all of creation for its own rebellious state. Indeed, the fact that He has not, is itself a miraculous display of His kindness and love toward each of us. We deserve nothing of His kindness and grace; yet, He has provided it to us anyway. Furthermore, He paid the penalty for our sins with the blood of His own son.

THE PLIGHT OF MANKIND IN THE HANDS OF PERFECT RIGHTEOUSNESS

To me belongeth vengeance and recompence; their foot shall slide in due time: for the day of their calamity is at hand, and the things that shall come upon them make haste. For the Lord shall judge his people (Deuteronomy 32:35-36).

As, I begin to gaze upon God's Glory, displayed in His perfect righteousness and justice; I must fall before Him prostrate. To consider that He would love, cherish and provide a way of salvation for me; forces my heart to praise Him. Only then, can I see the trials of this world as minuscule compared to the wrath I deserve.

For you see, sin fills my regenerate heart with not only those sins of commission; but also, those of omission. Were it not for God's Grace, I could never be a part of this His bigger story of joy, hope, love, and Glory. How I see the world changes; when I understand fully the majesty of His Grace, recognizing the truth that He IS perfect righteousness and justice. Instead of bemoaning what I have not received, I must praise Him and rejoice in what I am given.

Jonathan Edwards was a preacher in the early 1800s whose brilliant mind lead a revival throughout the land. One of his sermons stands as an example so clear concerning these truths from Deuteronomy 32. That sermon is titled *Sinners in the Hands of an Angry God.*

Effie Darlene Barba

QUOTES FROM JONATHAN EDWARDS "SINNERS IN THE HANDS OF AN ANGRY GOD"

That the reason why they are not fallen already and do not fall now is only that God's appointed time is not come. For it is said, that when that due time, or appointed time comes, their foot shall slide. Then they shall be left to fall, as they are inclined by their own weight. God will not hold them up in these slippery places any longer, but will let them go; and then, at that very instant, they shall fall into destruction. As he that stands on such slippery declining ground, on the edge of a pit, he cannot stand alone, when he is let go he immediately falls and is lost.

Unconverted men walk over the pit of hell on a rotten covering.

The bow of God's wrath is bent, and the arrow made ready on the string, and justice bends the arrow at your heart, and strains the bow. It is nothing but the mere pleasure of God, and that of an angry God, without any promise or obligation at all, that keeps the arrow one moment from being made drunk with your blood.[6]

CONCLUDING THOUGHTS

Knowing God IS perfect justice and righteousness, my heart transforms to see the magnitude of Grace He has given to me and to every human being born on this earth. Tragedies happen, not as a display of a merciless God; for evil would drown out any beauty of this world, were it not for God's Gracious hand steadying the course every day that this earth still orbits the sun. The entire world would fall into its own self-destruction, chaos, and despair; were it not for a gracious God who steadies His hand and holds it suspended by grace. The moment He lets go, this world will fall to destruction by its own weight of sin.

Every flower, every sunset, every gentle act of kindness that we see displayed in this world proclaims the grace of God toward this world and all who live here.

Were it not for Grace, there would never be glimpses of God's own perfect love being displayed by believers and nonbelievers alike. Instead, we would have plunged into utter darkness of our own making. Until we realize just as darkness is the absence of light, evil is the absence of good. God only is good; therefore, evil is the absence of God. Were He not displaying glimpses of His goodness, revealing His essence to us; evil would overtake this earth completely. Even those acts

---

[6] Jonathan Edwards, "Sinners in the Hands of an Angry God", *jonathan-edwards.org, accessed October 21, 2017. http://www.jonathan-edwards.org/Sinners.pdf.*

of kindness displayed by unbelievers come because of a gracious, loving God displaying His beauty and love to an underserving world. That is how big His love is. He even uses those who profane His name to display His love and grace to the world.

Chapter 7:

God IS LOVE

From the most fragile newborn, whose instinct is to nuzzle, to the lonely senior whose eyes light up by a visit; we are all born with a need to love and to be loved. Like a driving force deep within our psyche; we must recognize that we were created with this great need for love.

If indeed, we were just some chance of science; why would we be driven by such an in depth emotional need? The depth of loneliness cries out to us as a nation. Consider the suicide rate, the drug addictions, alcoholism, and the divorce rate. All point to our inability to fulfill our need to feel loved. No matter how much we think of love, believe in love, or chase after love; we find that often we are disappointed by our attempts at love. Even the mother who shares such devotion and love toward her child, at moments find that same love disappointing; because, there remains an aching in her heart that is not fully satisfied. At least, not all the time.

And yet, of all the emotions of human kind that are the hardest to explain by some co-incidental formation of cells as believed by the evolutionists, love is the most difficult to explain. Without some power much higher than ourselves; could we ever truly love another?

God, who created us, IS love and the only way to really know love is to know Him!

I am certain, there are a few skeptics out there who would say, "wait a minute. Haven't you seen atheists who love their children, their community, and their partners?" Of course, I have. So, how could I say to really know love; one must know God? The reality is that God's Grace is such that He taps on the shoulders of all men; precisely because of love. He displays this character of His Divine Nature to people; to draw them to Himself. Just as, God shares the beauty of His creation with all people; so, they might glimpse upon His Glorious beauty; He also displays His Divine Nature, by allowing people to experience love, so they might begin to realize, He IS. Nothing draws us closer to divinity than to experience true love.

Therefore, if God IS love; then, let's look at the characteristics of true love as shown in His Character of love, Calvary love, and His covenant love toward us.

CHARACTER OF LOVE

> *Love is patient and kind. Love is not jealous or boastful or proud or rude. It does not demand its own way. It is not irritable, and it keeps no record of being wronged. It does not rejoice about injustice but rejoices whenever the truth wins out. Love never gives up, never loses faith, is always hopeful, and endures through every circumstance. 1 Corinthians 13:4-7 (NLT)*

The Christian community knows that these verses are love's creed; which, we proclaim at many weddings or have hanging on our walls. Yet, by our own nature; we realize that we fail to fulfill these, just as often as we fail to fulfill the 10 commandments. God knew that we couldn't keep this or the

10 commandments without His Love filling our hearts to help us to perform. Which brings us to Calvary Love.

CALVARY LOVE

When Jesus hung on that cross, there is no way that He looked out upon the crowd who were mocking Him, who had beaten Him, and who screamed crucify Him with a thought of how lovely they are. I love them because of their beautiful hearts. NO! He saw their ugly, regenerate hearts; and, He loved them enough to say, "*Father, forgive them for they know not what they do!*"(Luke 23:44) He did not love them because they were so good, beautiful and lovely. Instead, He loved them because He knew that all who would accept His gift, would be transformed into receptacles of His love. He knew the vessels of love they would be to a world in need. In Him and through the power of His Love, they could become vessels which could transport His love to the world around them.

> *God commendeth his love toward us, in that, while we were yet sinners, Christ died for us. Much more then, being now justified by his blood, we shall be saved from wrath through him* (Romans 5:8-9).

There, on that cross, God saved us from the wrath of sin, by pouring out the just penalty of our sin on His Own Son; so that, we might then be the benefactors of His love and that we might really know love. He went a step further in that, He also provides for us His covenant love which assures that we cannot fall away from His love, having once accepted His gift of salvation.

COVENANT LOVE

Covenant love is a love of promise. I will not leave you, no matter what happens. My love will remain through every dark circumstance. I will love you when you are your most unlovely and when you don't even remember my love for you. When your faith fails you, I will be there to lift you up.

> *O LORD, the God of Israel, there is no God like You in heaven above or on earth beneath, keeping covenant and showing lovingkindness to Your servants who walk before You with all their heart* (1 King 8:23).

> *My covenant I (God) will not violate, Nor will I alter the utterance of My lips* (Psalm 89:34).

> *For the mountains may be removed and the hills may shake, But My lovingkindness will not be removed from you, And My covenant of peace will not be shaken," Says the LORD who has compassion on you* (Isaiah 54:10).

TO REALLY KNOW LOVE

The only way to really know love is to know God; because, God is love. When you accept His gift of love, as presented by His gift of Salvation; He will transform your heart so that you really know love. That love then reaches out from your own overflowing heart to all those around you.

Chapter 8:

The Great Lie

Finding steadfast joy in life begins with knowing your place in the Universe with promise. Faith comes from knowing God IS and God rewards those who diligently seek Him (Hebrews 11:6). Knowing this transforms our view of everything else in our life. No longer can I believe that life is by random chance, when, I believe that God IS Sovereign Creator, the Being without which no other being can exist; who rules supreme with righteousness, justice and love.

How can I question He who has promised to fit everything together for my good, who willingly moves all of heaven and earth; that I might see Him as my greatest treasure and find in Him my greatest joy! Furthermore, I have the choice to choose the Great lie of Satan, fighting for my own importance; or to begin anew with this truth: God IS.

I began this section declaring that the power to reject the null hypothesis of life, is knowing God IS--the Great I AM. The null hypothesis being the belief that everything is by chance. God IS the power to reject the null hypothesis; because His Sovereignty over my life, means nothing that happens in my life is by chance.

Then, we looked at Being and Nothingness. My being cannot fully exist outside of my Creator's pleasure for it to. Because my being is found in Him, I recognize my nothingness without Him.

We have explored some of the characteristics of God- -a part of His Being: Perfect Righteousness, Justice, and Love. Knowing these truths are central to our faith in Him and discovering our Place on this earth.

Furthermore, knowing our place comes with a promise of His providing all that we need by His great riches in Glory. He promises to Be all that we need, to guide us, transform us, and to bring us into His Joy with eternal life in Him. God IS our hope, our joy, our provider, our protector and our guide.

THE DESPAIRING GREAT LIE

Many in society believe and perpetuate the lie that happiness begins with individuals learning to stand firm on their own self-awareness. They want us to believe that the universe revolves around, "me". Humanistic Psychology has penetrated our society, our churches, and our schools. We are to be politically correct and do all that we can to build the self's ego; as though, each person is their own god. People believe this to be a new, evolved ideology; although, it is the same lie Satan told Eve.

Along with this ideology also arises the belief that if I positively believe I can "anything"; then, I would be certain to accomplish it. If only, I believe myself wealthy, I will be, etc. Again, this fits within the same lie that Adam and Eve fell for in the garden of Eden.

One of the gravest results of society's great lie comes when an individual faces their own frailties, and failures for the first time, or circumstances don't work out as planned. Because their hope was based upon a lie; fear, despair, and hopelessness becomes overwhelming. Lost within their quiet desperation, anxiety forces them to seek out safe places to try and hide, hoping to avoid conflict. Many times, the despair leads to either suicide, drug addiction, or violence.

Instead, when I know that my place is found in my realizing my own weakness and nothingness; then, I find my Being in God. In Him, I find purpose and newfound Position of Strength, Hope and Joy as His Beloved Child. Everything changes from hopelessness to great hope, quiet desperation to Joy, and nothingness to true Being; because, He gives me a new meaning for life.

C.S. LEWIS WROTE:

> *What Satan put into the heads of our remote ancestors was the idea that they could "be like gods"—could set up on their own as if they had created themselves—be their own masters— invent some sort of happiness for themselves outside God, apart from God. And out of that hopeless attempt has come nearly all that we call human history—money, poverty, ambition, war, prostitution, classes, empires, slavery—the long terrible story of man trying to find something other than God which will make him happy. God cannot give us a happiness and peace apart from Himself,*

Effie Darlene Barba

because it is not there. There is no such thing
C. S. Lewis, *Mere Christianity*[7]

The great lie has not changed over the ages. Indeed, we have merely given it a new name. Still the great lie cannot bring us contentment; because, happiness, peace, joy, love, beauty, and light do not exist except by the Grace of God that reaches out to all men. Because of Grace, He allows every one of us to see a glimpse of His truth and then allows us to choose Him or the great lie.

When I focus upon me, as though I am; I begin to focus on only my feelings, my desires, my pleasures, my success, and my importance. That always leads ultimately to a self-absorbed life; which ultimately leads to isolation and despair. Our modern positive thinking gurus say that it will lead to success. However, without God being the only I AM; the great lie leads to social chaos, despair, and failure. Indeed, that ideology led to the crumbling of many great societies over the course of history.

CHOOSING NOTHINGNESS, FINDING FULL BEING

In God, the opposite is true; because, God IS. Therefore, those who truly find steadfast joy both in this life and eternity are those who learn to embrace their own nothingness in this universe. Then, they find their being in God, by faith; because, He is the only true source of our

---

[7] C.S. Lewis, *Mere Christianity*, (New York: Macmillan, 1952), 53

being. This concept is in direct opposition of what society's great lie would tell you; because, society tells you your power comes by believing you are the center of all your world. You have a choice here! Choose God as Supreme Lord of your life; or continue believing the great lie that you are the center of your universe. Choosing God will lead to great happiness, joy, and hope. Otherwise, choosing the great lie leads to ultimate despair.

Jesus spoke these words which I want you to ponder:

MATTHEW 5:3-12

Blessed are the poor in spirit: for theirs is the kingdom of heaven. Blessed are they that mourn: for they shall be comforted. Blessed are the meek: for they shall inherit the earth. Blessed are they which do hunger and thirst after righteousness: for they shall be filled. Blessed are the merciful: for they shall obtain mercy. Blessed are the pure in heart: for they shall see God. Blessed are the peacemakers: for they shall be called the children of God. Blessed are they which are persecuted for righteousness' sake: for theirs is the kingdom of heaven. Blessed are ye, when men shall revile you, and persecute you, and shall say all manner of evil against you falsely, for my sake. Rejoice, and be exceeding glad: for great is your reward in heaven: for so persecuted they the prophets which were before you.

CONCLUDING THOUGHT BITES

Choose to believe the Great lie of Satan, fighting for your importance; or to begin anew with this truth: God IS

The great lie says 'I' am everything. Truth says GOD IS only in Him I am

Focusing on self-exaltation leads to a life of lonely despair, God exaltation brings love and joy

Out of the Nothingness

By Effie Darlene Barba

When I look in the mirror to gaze at my face

The scars deep within I cannot erase

The years that I tried to stand on my own

Wanting to be and to be known

I tried, oh so hard to do what was right

To struggle with all my strength and my might

Falling so short, I never could be

More than the darkness deep inside me

There where I saw the truth of my plight

Nothing in me could ever bring light

Into the darkness that shone all around

No hope to conquer as evils abound

Then when I knew there was nothing in me

That could calm the raging, roaring sea

You were the one who reached out Your hand

Showing me how in You I could stand

My LORD and King in Sovereignty Reign

Washing me clean of my guilty stain

That out of the nothingness that is me

You enter in that I might then be

The warrior You need to go to the fight

Telling the world of Your strength and might

While singing a song of joyous delight

Shining with truth in your glorious light

When I can see the world through your eyes

Trusting in You to make my heart wise

I become Nothing, that You then can be

The bright shining hope for the world to see

That out of the nothingness that is me

You enter in that I might then be

Effie Darlene Barba

Chapter 9:

A PLACE WITH PROMISE

Throughout this section of the book, I presented the case for finding our place in this Universe by first understanding this truth: God IS. The core fiber of our faith begins there; however, it does not end there; because as clearly stated in Hebrews 11: 6 *"he that cometh to God must believe that he is, and that he is a rewarder of them that diligently seek him"*.

So, it begins with knowing God IS Sovereign Lord, the Being that brings existence into our nothingness. God, filled with righteousness, justice, and love; IS fully in control and completes all that He has planned. Beyond that, He promises that "all things work together for good to those who love Him" (Romans 8:28). The entire word of God details God's promises of love, protection, provision, and fulfillment of joy in us and for us. Every trial we face guides us to know Him intimately. He IS the Powerful Promise of Hope for you and for me.

Jesus is our great shepherd providing for our every need who lovingly, willingly died and was resurrected from the dead to secure eternal life for us (John 10). Furthermore, He IS the one who holds our position secure in Him.

My sheep hear my voice, and I know them, and they follow me: And I give unto them eternal life; and they shall never perish, neither shall any man pluck them out of my hand. My Father, which gave them me, is greater than all; and no man is able to pluck

them out of my Father's hand. I and my Father
are one (John 10:27-30).

Having accepted Christ as my Savior, He holds me
secure; and, not even I can wander so far; but, that my Lord
and Master will draw me back into His arms of love.

POWERFUL PROMISE OF LOVE

Who shall separate us from the love of Christ?
shall tribulation, or distress, or persecution, or
famine, or nakedness, or peril, or sword? As it
is written, For thy sake we are killed all the day
long; we are accounted as sheep for the
slaughter. Nay, in all these things we are more
than conquerors through him that loved
us. For I am persuaded, that neither death, nor
life, nor angels, nor principalities, nor powers,
nor things present, nor things to come, Nor
height, nor depth, nor any other creature, shall
be able to separate us from the love of God,
which is in Christ Jesus our Lord (Romans
8:35-39).

No trial, no circumstance and no one can separate us
from the love of Christ Jesus. God, the Sovereign Creator
and Lord of this Universe, has given to all who will receive
His Gift of Salvation this promise for all of eternity. Once
you and I understand the truth that God IS; then, we can
believe His Powerful Promises of Hope. When I fully
KNOW this truth, how could I ever doubt or worry again; no
matter what storm I face! How could my heart ever again live
in quiet desperation: regardless of how bad the circumstances
that surround me.

POWERFUL PROMISE OF JOY

As Jesus was heading toward the garden of Gethsemane and nearing the time that he was to suffer upon the cross, he talked with His Father in heaven. "*And now come I to thee; and these things I speak in the world, that they might have my joy fulfilled in themselves*" (John 17:13).

Even before this prayer, Jesus had told His disciples, "*These things have I spoken unto you, that my joy might remain in you, and that your joy might be full.*"(John 15:11)

This is not some frivolous, fly by night joy; it is a steadfast, bubbling fountain of joy abiding deep within our souls. The Holy Spirit living in us, comforting us and reminding us of all the Heavenly Father has provided for us and all He has promised by Grace. *For the kingdom of God is not meat and drink; but righteousness, and peace, and joy in the Holy Ghost* (Romans 14:17). *But the fruit of the Spirit is love, joy, peace, longsuffering, gentleness, goodness, faith, Meekness, temperance* (Galatians 5:22-23).

POWERFUL PROMISE OF HOPE

So, how do I hold fast to the powerful promise of hope? All, I do is believe. Then, the God of hope does the rest. He, step by step; displays more glimpses of His Glory to me. Because He IS, I never face the storms alone. I can trust His plan to be that which is best for me. He IS the God of all hope, joy, love, and He loves me. That is all I need to know to face any trial or circumstance that comes my way.

Furthermore, when I truly KNOW deep within my heart that God IS in control and everything that He ordains for my life ultimately brings me closer to Him. Whatever, sorrow, heartbreak, pain or suffering that enters my life; God's loving hand sent, that I might grow closer to Him, lean deeper into Him; and thereby, find my joy complete in Him.

> *Now the God of hope fill you with all joy and peace in believing, that ye may abound in hope, through the power of the Holy Ghost* (Romans 15:13).

CONCLUDING THOUGHT BITES

Because God IS, I never face the storms alone. He is my hope and joy

Once we understand the truth that God IS; then, we can believe His Powerful Promises of Hope.

When we understand God IS and that He rewards those who diligently seek Him; then, we KNOW that all things work together for our best- His plan-nothing less, nothing more and nothing else can be the best for my life.

FOUNDATION 2

PURPOSE

Effie Darlene Barba

CHAPTER 10:

BROKEN, SEEKING PURPOSE

My heart lay shattered at my feet. Uncertain, whether my sorrow came more from the broken relationship; or from the guilt and shame of having broken God's command. Although, I daresay, this time; unlike the others, reflected more my broken spirit from having brought shame to my heavenly Father's Name. How could I not learn from before? Why did I allow myself to fall into the trap, believing Satan's lie that after all, God would understand my loneliness and need for intimacy? Or the other lie, that maybe this was the best God had for me, anyway. I, so underserving, would settle for less.

Once more, I had poured out my heart, my soul; giving love with every ounce of my being, compromising my convictions. How many times had I promised God, that I would be better and wouldn't let this happen again. Now, here I was again; let behind, alone with my own failures. I loved God; but, I just couldn't seem to get this one thing right. Broken, defeated and filled with sorrow, I didn't even know what to pray. I feared making any more promises; because, I knew that I couldn't keep them.

My entire life, I heard that my purpose as a Christian was to bring God Glory; and though, I had longed to do that, I had tried with every ounce of my body; I had failed again. Now I realized, I brought shame, not Glory, to the name of God. All the good I did, destroyed by my own sin. How could God still love me? What in the world could be my purpose now? There I lay in the ashes of my own guilt and shame.

PURPOSE-If Not to Bring God Glory, then What?

There I lay in the depth of my own despair. I read a book called, *When We Get It Wrong* by Dominic Smart. That book reminded me that when God reached out to touch the heart of a 5-year-old girl and bid her come, He knew every time I would fail Him and He loved me, chose me and saved me all the same. That truth guided me to continue seeking to know even more, asking God for His wisdom to show me how to honor Him.

As He taught me, I ultimately shared what I had learned in a book I wrote, *A Broken and Contrite Heart.* That made me begin to question the idea of my purpose being to bring God Glory. After all, even if I could get it all right and follow every command perfectly; there was nothing that I could do that would bring one iota of Glory to Perfect Gory.

Therefore, I began to wonder; what then could be my purpose in life. I asked God to reveal this to me. What He then revealed became the second great foundational truth of life needed to be able to find steadfast, abiding joy. In fact, it became key to learning how to have victory as well.

GOD'S PURPOSE: John 17

One day while reading John 17, I realized God's purpose for creating me and saving me was quite different than I had ever thought before. Suddenly a light of hope, joy and power surged into my own darkness as I realized God created me to be a receptacle of His Love, His Joy and His Glory. It had nothing to do with my power to do; rather, the more I emptied myself of me, the more love, joy and reflections of glory would be mine. Furthermore, God could use the cracks and brokenness of this vessel to pour out His Grace to a world in need of Him.

There within this prayer, Jesus stated clearly our purpose to become the receptacles of God's Love, Joy, and vessels through which His Glory would shine, (not ours, but His).

> *These words spake Jesus, and lifted up his eyes to heaven, and said, Father, the hour is come; glorify thy Son, that thy Son also may glorify thee: As thou hast given him power over all flesh, that he should give eternal life to as many as thou hast given him...And now come I to thee; and these things I speak in the world, that they might have my joy fulfilled in themselves... Sanctify them through thy truth: thy word is truth... And the glory which thou gavest me I have given them; that they may be one, even as we are one:.. I in them, and thou in me, that they may be made perfect in one; and that the world may know that thou hast sent me, and hast loved them, as thou hast loved me.* (John 17:1-2,13,17,22-23).

In other words, God's purpose for my life was that He would pour upon me His Joy, His love, and His Glory; while sanctifying me through His word of truth; because of the atoning sacrifice of Jesus Christ for me. It had nothing to do with my working to bring Him Glory; it had everything to do with His transforming work in me and through me by His Grace and love toward me.

No longer did I need to live in quiet desperation over my past, my failures and my inability to bring Him Glory; because, that had never been the purpose for which He created me.

A CHANGE OF FOCUS

When I begin to understand the purpose of my life from God's viewpoint; then, I learn to sit at His feet, in His presence to receive all that I need to face every obstacle that lies before me. When my purpose changes from my accomplishments to His accomplishments through me; then, I forcibly lay aside all pride and all selfish desires for personal Glory or fame. My prayer becomes, "God, Your Will, Nothing More, Nothing Less and Nothing Else."[8] Furthermore, when I realize I was created that God might shower upon me His Love, His Joy and pour forth over me His Glory; then, I see the circumstances of this world in a different light. No longer do I view things through the imperfect lenses of my eyes. Instead, I begin to see life through the eyes of Jesus.

Then, once my focus changes; I clearly see the depth of grace God displays in my life purpose. When I see my

---

[8] Bobby Richardson, "Prayer at Fellowship of Christian Athletes", quoted on pastorterryblog., accessed on October 21,2017,
https://pastorterryblog.wordpress.com/2010/02/28/sunday-sermon-your-will-nothing-more-nothing-less-nothing-else.

purpose, fully as God's act of Grace; then, I humbly reach out to others with that same kind of Grace. Because I recognize my own inability to live this Christian life; then, I can humbly reach out with God's love to others who are entrapped by their own sin.

This does not provide me with a license to sin: quite the opposite. In fact, because I understand the truth of purpose; I find I sin less now than when I strove to Glorify God by my own might.

A JOURNEY TO PURPOSE

So, as we begin this journey to explore our purpose on earth; let us stop, for a moment and pray that God enlighten our hearts and minds to His truth. I need a God focus; rather than a me focus. I pray God help you understand this truth through His Scripture and through examples from my life story; which, I will share with you with as much transparency and vulnerability as God directs me to do.

It all begins with accepting God's Gift of Salvation as provided by His Son. Following this, we begin a journey of growing in Christ and being transformed by Him. Christ is always about the work of transforming His bride to become more beautiful with each day that passes. God has a purpose for our life. That purpose includes transforming our hearts that we might be able to experience a greater joy than we have ever known; because, God is Joy. His purpose is to mold us so that we may be able to experience love is a way we have never known before as His love fills us. And last for not least He is forming our testimony so that He might use it to win others to Him. When He does that; He shares a piece of His glory with me. For me that journey lead me down many winding and sometimes dark roads. Each road stretching me and opening my eyes to see the truth. I needed a new transformed heart that saw my purpose as relative to God's Purpose for me.

ISAIAH 14:24,26,27

> *The Lord of hosts hath sworn, saying, Surely as I have thought, so shall it come to pass; and as I have purposed, so shall it stand. This is the purpose that is purposed upon the whole earth: and this is the hand that is stretched out upon all the nations. For the Lord of hosts hath purposed, and who shall disannul it? and his hand is stretched out, and who shall turn it back?*

CONCLUDING THOUGHTS

My stumbling feet and stuttering speech could not in my own strength ever bring Glory to God. So, I needed to know His Purpose for me!

God's purpose for me will be accomplished by the power and might of His hand, no one can stop Him from completing His purpose in me. Not even me.

CHAPTER 12:

FROM VICTIMS TO WARRIORS

Purpose is defined as the reason for which something is done, created or exists. Therefore, knowing one's true purpose drives one's actions. Furthermore, understanding the purpose for my life existence, infuses me with the power that transforms me from Victim to Warrior in every situation of life.

When God revealed to me His true purpose for my life as a receptacle of His Joy, Love and Glory; my focus changed from what I could do for God to what God could do through me. Furthermore, my heart transformed from being a victim of my own self, to becoming a warrior ready and willing to fight against sin.

If (as some wrongly believe) I exist to perform acts for God which are impossible to do on my own; then, I will be always in a rollercoaster state of striving and giving up. On the other hand, if my purpose is to be a receptacle of God's love, joy and Glory; then, I willingly, joyously accept whatever process God sends to empty me of my pride, arrogance, and selfish desire. When I grasp the full magnitude of His wonderous purpose for my life, He becomes the goal. Then, above all else; my desire is to know Him fuller, spending time in His presence and embracing His Will for my life--no matter what! Furthermore, when I recognize His Being; the more evident becomes my nothingness. Recognizing He has the best plan for me, I surrender to His Will Joyfully. The more I know of Him, the more I desire to know. Instead of a rollercoaster ride of ups and downs; I begin to see a steady upward climb pressing toward Glory, which is God in the face of Jesus Christ shining forth to me.

Effie Darlene Barba

FROM VICTIM TO WARRIOR

There was an aboding sense of fear deep within my heart until that moment I knew, this was God's plan. My father's eyes filled with tears; yet, he helped me to pack my car and load the children into their car seats. Six months earlier, I had arrived home; planning to start over. Defeated, tired, I bore the scars and bruises of domestic abuse. Accomplished as a nurse; able to make my own living--certainly, I was not your usual victim of abuse. I had options. So, why did I return? Before you think I am telling women to remain in abuse; let me say, that I would tell anyone to run as fast as they can; unless, as was my case, God clearly says, Go back.

The first 5 or 6 years of our marriage, I was a victim; because, of why I remained. Believing that perhaps everything was my fault, I tried harder each day to be a better wife, better mother, better housekeeper, and just better. That was exhausting. I struggled with all my might to be better and could not get it right, or so I thought. My entire goal was to gain the love of this man; whom I felt unworthy of. He was smart, handsome, and cultured. I was a country girl, plain and simple. A part of me believed everything was my fault. That was when I truly was a victim. However, when I returned; I was God's Warrior. A gentle, kind loving warrior; but, a strong and mighty warrior all the same. And so it was, that Christian children's songs played in my cassette player as I and my sons sang along; while we traveled from Dexter, MO back to Dallas, Texas that day.

WHEN TRUTH DEFINES PURPOSE; REASON CHANGES EVERYTHING

During the time away, I had grown to realize two things: I was God's beloved child and, as such perfected by the atoning work of Jesus Christ on the cross. Because of being God's Beloved, Blessed and redeemed Child, I recognized and heard that still small voice bidding me to return. Part of me did not want to go, at first. I argued with God for months; then, I realized that God had a bigger plan and ultimately that plan would be for my good. God filled my heart with an unconditional love, as I began to see the truth of Pete's heart through God's eyes. Beyond that, I saw in Pete, an injured child; desperately in need of healing. The nurturing nature God placed in the heart of this mother and nurse, could not walk away.

Once more, let me be clear! In most cases of domestic abuse, that is not the case! Many are just plain evil forces that will not be transformed; but, I knew in my case, it was different, because, God said, "Go!"

Returning with purpose to do God's will and knowing that God loved me perfectly; I was no longer a victim. I was on a mission. That changed everything. My purpose had changed, when I let go of my will and followed God's Will.

WHEN TIMES GET ROUGH

The next 9 years I cannot lie and say were easy. Many times, I cried out to God, pleading for a different plan. Yet, God replied, "I am here with you every step of the way, my child." Never again, did I fear, even when a gun pointed at my head; because, I knew God stood firm as my protector, provider, and my guide. Ultimately, Pete found Christ as His Savior; then, God took Him home. Ah, but you see! God's plan was the salvation of one soul for an eternity with Him. What did that have to do with God's plan for my life? Everything!

LESSONS LEARNED THAT LEAD TO STRENGTH AND JOY

During those years, I learned of God's absolute complete unconditional love toward me. Because if God could transform my human heart to love unconditionally another human being; then, how much greater was God's unconditional love for me. I learned more of faith, hope, love and joy in Christ; during and through those years. Despite my having many more lessons to learn along this journey; for now, He had taught me to be fearless when following His command, no matter what.

Ultimately, I also learned

1.   There is no sacrifice too great for the salvation of one soul
2.   My strength, my hope and my joy rest within God's abiding presence in my life
3.   God's unconditional love for me stands stronger than any force of evil in this world.
4.   God holds me firmly in the palm of His Righteous right hand; therefore, I have nothing to fear.

EPHESIANS 1:9-14 (TLB)

God has told us his secret reason for sending Christ, a plan he decided on in mercy long ago; and this was his purpose: that when the time is ripe he will gather us all together from wherever we are—in heaven or on earth—to be with him in Christ forever. Moreover, because of what Christ has done, we have become gifts to God that he delights in, for as part of God's sovereign plan we were chosen from the beginning to be his, and all things happen just as he decided long ago.

God's purpose in this was that we should praise God and give glory to him for doing these mighty things for us, who were the first to trust in Christ.

And because of what Christ did, all you others too, who heard the Good News about how to be saved, and trusted Christ, were marked as belonging to Christ by the Holy Spirit, who long ago had been promised to all of us Christians.

His presence within us is God's guarantee that he really will give us all that he promised; and the Spirit's seal upon us means that God has already purchased us and that he guarantees to bring us to himself. This is just one more reason for us to praise our glorious God.

Effie Darlene Barba

CHAPTER 12:

HOW CAN ANYONE REJECT PERFECT LOVE?

Have you ever loved someone dearly with all your heart, only to have that love rejected? The desperate agonizing feeling when you come to realize the truth, the nauseating sensation in the pit of your stomach, and the despair that follows; all because, they did not see or accept your gift of love. You would have sacrificed anything, just to make them happy; but, alas, they turned their back and walked away. Or perhaps a friend, a parent, or even a child; who despite the love you poured out upon them, returned disdain and spewed hate toward you instead. Imagine this, God created the world and humanity that He might lavish His love upon a people; instead, the clear majority have turned their backs upon that love, spewed hate filled words, sought after other loves, and rejected the greatest gift that He could give-eternity in the presence of perfect love.

God created the heavens and earth, with all that therein lies to shower His love upon a people. He created us with a body, soul, and spirit with which we could feel the emotional impact of love and joy. We could see splendor, beauty and the exuberance of Glory. His Divine Purpose was to shower us with love, fill us with His joy, and to share with us His Glory. Yet, for us to experience the fullness of His Glorious Being, we were given choice. Just as I cannot know the splendor of light, without having experienced darkness; neither can I understand God's perfect Righteousness or Justice, without having seen the absence of righteousness. Evil is the absence of righteousness. Perhaps, Adam had not fully realized what he had; until, it was gone. Adam had walked each day in the garden with God. He had God's love lavished upon him. Never had Adam been without joy!

REJECTED

That fate filled day, Adam chose to reject the truth of God. Thusly, Adam rejected God's gift of love. Instead, he chose to eat from the one tree that God had commanded him to not eat; the tree of the knowledge of good and evil. Until that moment, Adam had never known of evil. Perhaps, he could not understand the depth of love, nor righteousness that God IS; until that moment that he rejected God's command and lost the spiritual union with God. Despite the slap in the face of rejection, God's plan would march on toward providing a way that all who would accept His gift of love; could find perfect peace, joy, and hope in Him. Even before the earth was formed, God knew the choice Adam would make and God loved you and I enough to endure millenniums of hate; so that you and I might be recipients of His love, joy and glory.

Imagine this! God loves you so much; that He gave everything, just for you and I to have a chance to enjoy His pleasures for an eternity with Him. Still, so often; we go about life as discontented brides seeking other lovers to fulfill us; never recognizing, that we have all that we could ever need in Him.

THE STORY OF HOSEA

Hosea, a prophet of God; married an adulteress woman. God ordained that Hosea would love with a perfect love this woman; despite, her constant adulteress affairs. At one point in the story, she leaves him to care for the children alone, while she leads a life of prostitution. Yet, he loves her so much that when she is completely destitute from her life of prostitution; he gently brings her home to provide and care for her every need. This story illustrated the love God has for His people. The prophet Hosea lived the agonizing pain of being rejected by the woman he loved; so that, he fully understood and passionately told the nation of Israel of God's love. This was indeed a picture of God's love for His people. This story was to the Israelite nation; but, the same is true for all the inhabitants of this earth. All are given the choice to receive God's love or to reject it.

Christ came to this earth to seal the promise. Those in the old testament believed in His coming to redeem the world and we look back to His finished work. Both, are given the opportunity to either receive or reject that love. To all who will, God declares:

> *And I will betroth thee unto me forever; yea,*
> *I will betroth thee unto me in righteousness,*
> *and in judgment, and in lovingkindness, and*
> *in mercies. I will even betroth thee unto me in*
> *faithfulness: and thou shalt know the LORD*
> (Hosea 2:19-20).

A CHOICE FOR LOVE

When you fully see the depth, breadth, and height of God's love for you; how, can you still reject it? Yet, so many do just that. If you understand the truth that God loves you with an everlasting love, why would you ever feel depressed or sad? Knowing that God IS Sovereign and He loves you with a perfect love, how could you not trust Him with every detail of your life?

The LORD hath appeared of old unto me, saying, Yea, I have loved thee with an everlasting love: therefore, with lovingkindness have I drawn thee (Jeremiah 31:3).

Just as Jesus wept over Jerusalem, so does He weep over every one of you who have rejected His call.

O Jerusalem, Jerusalem, which killest the prophets, and stonest them that are sent unto thee; how often would I have gathered thy children together, as a hen doth gather her brood under her wings, and ye would not! (Luke 13:34).

CHAPTER 13
OUT OF DEVASTATING LOSS INTO PERFECT JOY

Alone, broken-hearted; I wept bitterly through the night. After all the years of what I thought was serving God, here I lay. Not only was I alone; having been betrayed by my own search for love. Now, I faced betrayal at work. The one place where I had diligently served and had rose to a place of respect: the only place I believed I was loved. Perhaps I had grown too proud of my position. After all, it brought me great joy to know everyone looked up to me (or so I had thought until now). I had fought for Christ so many years; or so, I believed. Yet, there still were all those "if only" thoughts that would plague me at times. If only I were successful, or had more money, or was a little thinner. And of course, my old enemy returned to plague my brain; if only someone loved me: then, I could be happy. When Satan has knocked you to the curb; he starts whispering his old lies, knowing you are most vulnerable. He presents you with the same temptations you thought you had defeated.

Happiness and joy appeared in my life like a see saw: one moment up and the next crashing to the ground. This time, the down came with a crushing blow. The one place, I always excelled had been at work. Now, I was the accused; pronounced condemned, without so much a question or trial. Months went by and in fact, I resigned and I started my move to Missouri from Florida before everything was cleared up. Still, I felt a sadness deep within, from the feeling of rejection and hurt.

Well, back up a few months. Five months prior to this happening, I had known, without a shadow of a doubt,

God was commanding me to move to Missouri. There were many mountains in my way of moving. So, fasting and praying; I was waiting for God to move all the mountains first to make a clear pathway. Instead, there was this; which forced my hand to not wait any longer and to follow His command with all the mountains looming before me. I had to make a leap of faith to resign and prepare my move before I even had a job to go to. God, being faithful; worked out all the rest, after I began the preparation to move. Miraculously, the start date of the new job was one week after I completed the ninety days required in my contract.

After arriving in Missouri, God left me with a part time job where I faced many difficulties, criticisms, and struggles at first. My applications for a second job marked denied. Never had I faced rejections of this kind before. Suddenly my last stronghold of self-pride, crumbled within me. I now had to stand firm on God's promise that this was where He sent me and He would work out the rest.

SOURCE OF TRUE JOY

One by one, throughout my lifetime; God had ripped from my hands the counterfeit joys I clung to. He needed me to realize: He IS my joy. Happiness and joy did not depend upon all these things I thought I desired or believed I needed. Nor did they depend on my obtaining these. Many times, in my life, when facing disaster; I seemed to know this, only to let that truth slip quickly away again as I reached for or held too tightly to some new desire or string of pride. Why was it that I would lay aside the truth of True Joy to cling once more to counterfeit joys? My time alone with God would slide; just a little. Busy with other things, I stopped reading my Bible. Preoccupied with some new counterfeit joy, I left my only True Joy laying in some corner.

Then, God would snatch that counterfeit joy out of my hand; and, once more I would fall into despair. Only, in the center of my tears; I would look up to see God there in all His Glory. His loving arms were there to pull me up; lift me out of my sorrow. Then, His joy would fill my heart again.

The problem! We fail to understand this truth: the purpose for which God created us was to shower us with His love, fill us with His Joy, and bestow upon us His Glory. When we lose sight of our purpose, we seek all these things through self-made means. Because I seek love, joy, and glory; I search for it through whatever means I can. Much like Adam, I tend to forget: I already have all of it when I sit in His presence.

KNOWLEDGE THAT TRANSFORMS

When I understand fully that God IS, that He rewards those who seek Him, and that my purpose in this life is to be a receptacle of His love, joy and Glory; then, everything changes. Because I begin to see the world through God's eyes, I begin to know Joy in the center of every trial. I know that He is the Joy I was searching for. Therefore, I set my alarm to get up at 4 am every morning to spend time alone with Him. Beyond that, I seek His presence with whispered prayers of "thank you, Lord", "guide me Lord" and "Your Will, Lord" throughout my day. Praise, worship songs and sermons surround me in my car and as I work around my house.

Thou wilt keep him in perfect peace, whose mind is stayed on thee: because he trusteth in thee. Trust ye in the Lord forever: for in the Lord Jehovah is everlasting strength (Isaiah 26:3-4).

Thou wilt shew me the path of life: in thy presence is fulness of joy; at thy right hand there are pleasures for evermore (Psalm 16:11).

JEREMIAH 29:11-13

For I know the thoughts that I think toward you, saith the Lord, thoughts of peace, and not of evil, to give you an expected end. Then shall ye call upon me, and ye shall go and pray unto me, and I will hearken unto you. And ye shall seek me, and find me, when ye shall search for me with all your heart.

Note this: God's ultimate plan is that we seek Him; because (Richardson 1010) He knows our only hope for everlasting Joy is found in Him. After all, He created us for that precise purpose. Another very important lesson is that of Charles Stanley's motto: "Obey God and leave all the consequences to Him."[9]

---

[9]Charles Stanley, "Life Principle 2: A Life of Obedience," *Intouch.org.* July 2, 2014, accessed October 2, 2017, https://www.intouch.org/read/life-principle-2-a-life-of-obedience.

THE STORY'S CONCLUSION: JOY OVERFLOWING

Six months after my arrival in Missouri, my situation took a sharp turn toward all that God had planned for me. My part time job went to full time. Richly blessed, I work with two of the best and kindest Electrophysiology Physicians in the world at the VA. Honored to be led by a great group of Cardiologists, my life beams with hope and joy. God has shined His light upon me. What a blessing to be able to serve the Veterans alongside a very dedicated and caring staff, which we have here.

God knew that I would have hesitated leaving Florida; had, He not created a storm there. He knew that He had His best for me here where I am now; therefore, He ripped from my hand a counterfeit joy that I might find true joy in the center of His will and plan for me. No longer was I relying on me or my accolades to find joy; instead, He IS my joy. All the rest of my happy benefits are bonus.

CONCLUDING THOUGHTS

Remember the beginning of this page! "Alone, broken-hearted; I wept bitterly through the night. After all the years of what I thought was serving God, here I was. Not only was I alone" How quickly does our own thought process get messed up when we take our eyes off our only true source of joy! You, see: I was never alone; because God was right there with me every step of the way. Furthermore, perhaps, I believed that my serving God deserved some trophy or reward; when, the truth is: my sin filled pride filled heart deserved nothing but condemnation. Despite that, I had always had Him at my side, as my greatest treasure because of His Grace, not anything I could do with my own strength. His presence was mine and did not depend on my own futile attempts at serving Him. Without Him, I had no hope. He IS my strength, my hope and my joy!

When I remember the truth of my place within this universe (nothing without Him) and my purpose to be God's receptacle for love, joy and glory; then, I am filled with and amazed by steadfast, abiding Joy. No matter what comes, I am undaunted by the storms; because, He IS ALL I need. No longer can my life be one of quiet desperation.

CONCLUDING THOUGHT BITES

God ripped from my hand a counterfeit joy that I might find true joy in Him

No longer relying on me or my accolades to find joy; God IS my joy.

God created us with purpose, so He could fill us with His Joy & bestow His Love on us

Chapter14:

Ascending to the Edge of Glory

Along with our inner desire for love and happiness, there dwells within each heart the desire to succeed. Deep within our being, there is a longing for Glory; because, everyone is born with the desire to seek Glory in one way or another. We long for things of beauty and excellence. We yearn to belong and be a part of that which is eternal. This is true of everyone; even, the atheist wants to leave some indelible mark on this world, so that his legacy lives on. All too often, we want to know the how to ascend to the Edge of Glory; without wondering about the who or the why.

Our purpose becomes skewed; as we see the end as more important than the means. Precisely, the reason so many Christians are also deceived into believing we were created that we might bring God Glory; instead of realizing, that He graciously wants to share with us His Glory.

There is a very fine distinction between the two. The idea that I might bring God Glory, focuses on me and my accomplishments. Self-focus can, during moments of success, bring elation and joy. However, it brings great despair; whenever, we fail to succeed. After all, with so many people on the planet; we cannot all be number 1, all the time. Sometimes, we win and at other times we may lose. Often, because others and we, ourselves become focused on personal achievement, we become obsessed with our failures. Then, we turn to lives of quiet desperation, feeling rejected, lonely and inadequate. It is no wonder our society is plagued by depression, addictions, suicides, anger and selfishness.

We are drowning in an ocean of hearts seeking Glory, without understanding true purpose. Furthermore, ashamed to admit the critical tapes in our own heads, we push on: wanting success, wanting to find the edge of Glory.

A SHIFT IN FOCUS

Isaiah tells us of a moment in time he gazed upon God's Glory.

In the year that king Uzziah died I saw also the Lord sitting upon a throne, high and lifted up, and his train filled the temple. Above it stood the seraphims: each one had six wings; with twain he covered his face, and with twain he covered his feet, and with twain he did fly. And one cried unto another, and said, Holy, holy, holy, is the Lord of hosts: the whole earth is full of his glory (Isaiah 6:1-3).

Seeing a glimpse of Glory, Isaiah realized the depth of his own depravity and that of humanity.

Then said I, Woe is me! for I am undone; because I am a man of unclean lips, and I dwell in the midst of a people of unclean lips: for mine eyes have seen the King, the Lord of hosts (Isaiah 6:5).

Suddenly, Isaiah recognized his predicament. He was fully aware of his own failures, the darkness of his prideful heart, and his utter inability to bring any glory to Ultimate Glory.

GRACE THAT ASCENDS TO THE EDGE OF GLORY

God did not leave Isaiah there; broken with despair. Instead, God reached out to touch Isaiah with grace.

> Then flew one of the seraphims unto me, having a live coal in his hand, which he had taken with the tongs from off the altar: And he laid it upon my mouth, and said, Lo, this hath touched thy lips; and thine iniquity is taken away, and thy sin purged. Also, I heard the voice of the Lord, saying, whom shall I send, and who will go for us? Then said I, "Here am I; send me" (Isaiah 6:6-8).

Obviously, God could be His own spokesman. He really did not need Isaiah to be His messenger; however, God chose Isaiah. In one act of Grace, God chose to share a piece of His Glory with Isaiah. Isaiah would by one Gracious act of God be allowed to ascend to the edge of Glory. Every Jewish and Christian Scholar know the name of Isaiah; not, because of who Isaiah was. Rather, we all know the name of Isaiah; because of who God IS.

THE MYSTERY TRANSFORMING GLORY

Even the mystery which hath been hid from ages and from generations, but now is made manifest to His saints: To whom God would make known what is the riches of the glory of this mystery among the Gentiles; which is

Effie Darlene Barba

Christ in you, the hope of glory: (Colossians 1:26-27).

The mystery of our having any hope of Glory, can only be found in Christ Jesus. His Glory shining forth. I bring no Glory of my own to this equation. Understanding this truth, the mystery of how God can use imperfect men and women to display His Glory; transforms everything. God can and will use your life, your experiences, and your story to transform lives. When you look behind you; then, you will be amazed by the beauty and glory He has created from the rough, hard times in your life. Life gains new meaning. Hope reigns supreme. And, Joy will overflow into rivers. You will arise with newness of life every day. Freed from the chains of your own negative voices, you will be dancing.

Suddenly, you will find your life transforming as you seek Him more with each passing day. Success will abound around you. You may not be blessed with fame and fortune; but, you will be a success. God knows best whether you can deal with worldly success or not; therefore, He will guide your life, as He knows best. Either way, He will cause you to ascend to the edge of Glory.

PROMISE OF GLORY GIVEN BY JESUS

Jesus prayed to the Father, concerning all who would receive Him as Savior,

And the glory which You gave Me I have given them, that they may be one just as We are one: I in them, and You in Me; that they may

be made perfect in one, and that the world
may know that You have sent Me, and have
loved them as You have loved Me (John
17:22-23 NKJV).

When you and I recognize that our purpose is much
bigger than ourselves; we, like Isaiah cry out, "Here am I, send
me." We cannot fail; when, God takes the steering wheel of
our life. He will always steer us to the edge of Glory--His
Glory poured over our lives.

So, how does one ascend to the edge of Glory? By
realizing our place in this world and finding our purpose. Our
place: Nothingness without Him, fullness of Being in Him;
because God IS the Being without which nothing else
exists. His promise is to reward all who diligently seek
Him. Within that promised reward lies our purpose. He
created us that He might shower us with His love, bestow
upon us His Joy, and impart to us a part of His Glory. My
purpose becomes clear in the why and the who of my
purpose. It is all about Him, His Will: nothing more, nothing
less, and nothing else.

CONCLUDING THOUGHT BITES

We cannot fail; when, God takes the steering wheel of
our life.

God will always steer us to the edge of Glory--His
Glory poured over our lives.

When we realize our purpose is bigger than our self,
we are freed to ascend to the edge of Glory

We are drowning in an ocean of hearts seeking Glory, without understanding true purpose

CHAPTER 15:

A HIGHER PURPOSE

The reason or purpose why we do things, is more important than what we do. Dietrich Bonhoeffer understood his stance against Adolf Hitler and the Nazi Reich could cost him his life; but, he marched on. Because he saw a higher purpose than himself, he fought against the regime. For this, he faced imprisonment and death. Perhaps you might say, this is an extreme example of a higher purpose. Yet, this driving force against injustice began years before as a seed in his heart. He studied in the US for a time and fell in love with the Black Church. He hated the injustice plaguing our country during those years. That seed of seeking a higher purpose than his own comfort grew. In 1933, when Hitler rose to power; Dietrich Bonhoeffer was willing to fight; because, he knew his purpose was greater than his own comfort.

There are a lot of books, seminars and thoughts surrounding the idea of purpose. Often, others tell us purpose is something we drive our hearts and minds to obtain. If only I could change my reason; then, I will gain what I wanted. Can I change my heart? Or is that something much bigger than I?

GOD SAID:

This is the covenant that I will make with them after those days, saith the Lord, I will put my laws into their hearts, and in their minds will I

*write them; And their sins and iniquities will I
remember no more* (Hebrews 10:16-17).

And the Lord thy God

*will circumcise thine heart, and the heart of
thy seed, to love the Lord thy God with all
thine heart, and with all thy soul, that thou
mayest live* (Deuteronomy 30:6).

Don't miss this! God is the one who transforms our
hearts from the inside out. No amount of work that I strive
to do can change my heart. I cannot change my purpose on
my own without His guiding hand to change me. My only
hope is to turn to Him who can transform me; including, His
transforming my motives. When I surrender to the truth, I
become a receptacle of His plan. He created me to receive
His love and His joy as a gift of grace. Then, as I grow in my
relationship with Him; recognizing this truth, He creates the
path wherein He shares His Glory with me by using my
testimony to shine a light into the darkness of another's
heart. He does this by transforming my purpose from a me
centered life to a God centered life. All the Glory is His.

Only when I recognize my nothingness without Him,
can I find my Being in Him. My part? I am to seek
Him. Even in that, I must recognize my inadequacy to do so
without His help.

LIVING A HIGHER PURPOSE LIFE

So how can you find a life fully engaged in a higher purpose?

1. Acknowledge to God, you need His help and guidance to achieve your best life in Him. This begins with prayer.
2. Study His word
3. Listen closely, as your heart is drawn into a deeper relationship with Him
4. Awaken each morning at least 30 minutes early to be alone with Him.
5. Be Amazed by the Joy, peace, and hope overtaking your heart.
6. Thank Him for all He has done
7. Be Amazed again when you realize that His love, joy, and hope is overflowing to others around you.

THE GAIN EXCEEDS THE COST

Costly grace is the gospel which must be sought again and again and again, the gift which must be asked for, the door at which a man must knock. Such grace is costly because it calls us to follow, and it is grace because it calls us to follow Jesus Christ. It is costly because it costs a man his life, and it is grace because it gives a man the only true life. It is costly because it condemns sin, and grace because it justifies the sinner. Above all, it is costly because it cost God the life of his Son: 'Ye were bought at a price', and what has cost God much cannot be cheap for us. Above all, it is grace because God did not reckon his Son too dear a price to pay for our life, but delivered him up for us.[10]

At first and often along the way, Satan whispers to you; "You fool. You are wasting your time helping others, sacrificing your own happiness for others, giving up your vacation to lift another up, forsaking your comfort to give of your time to missions." Then, you can turn quickly and say, "Satan, your foolish counterfeit joys will never compare to the riches I have in Christ Jesus. He fills my heart with joy, hope, love and life. So, if you don't mind-shut up. If you do mind, shut up anyway."

CONCLUDING THOUGHT BITES

Turn quickly & say, "Satan, your counterfeit joys can't compare to my riches in Christ Jesus"

When I surrender to the truth, I become a receptacle of His plan.

God transforms my purpose from a me centered one to a God centered purpose

Higher Purpose begins as a seed that when nourished grows into a fruit bearing vine

---

[10] Dietrich Bonhoeffer, *The Cost of Discipleship,* trans. R.H. Fuller, (New York, NY: Touchstone, 1955), 45.

CHAPTER 16:

3 Foundations: Steadfast Joy

Abiding, steadfast joy penetrating the core of our hearts, no matter what storms arise in our lives. Isn't that what we want? That steady, unfailing hope allowing us to get up and move forward one step at a time. Strength arising from knowing all is well, guiding our thoughts and minds and driving out all anxiety and depression. You might say, "Impossible!" I would have said the same; until, God changed my views of life. He did so with many storms. Some were a result of my own failures and inadequacies, lacking the understanding I needed to stand firm. At other times, God sent unexpected storms; because He knew, through each one, in His Steady Guiding Hand was leading me to know Him better, closer. There, through the storms, I discovered the three truth foundations which give abiding, steadfast joy in life.

Through the previous chapters, we have looked at foundational truths #1 and #2 on which we may stand so that our lives can be filled with abiding, steadfast joy.

1. Knowing our Place in the Universe with Promise. This truth found in Hebrews 11:6; defines faith. Faith is knowing God IS and that He rewards those who diligently seek Him. Recognizing our own nothingness before an Almighty, Sovereign God (Creator of Heaven and Earth); we also realize He is the Being without which nothing else exists. Coupling this with His promise to reward those who diligently seek Him, we rest assured that "All things (no matter how bad they may look at first) ALL Things work

together for good to those who love God" Romans 8:28.

2. Knowing the purpose for which we were created. We were made for a much higher purpose of Glory; yet, because of sin we cannot achieve this in our own strength. No matter how hard I strive; pride and the need for self-exaltation stands in the way of truly living with higher purpose. Only by first recognizing my place of nothingness as I gaze upon the Almighty, Righteous King; can I become the receptacle of His Joy and Love. Beyond that, God shares a part of His Glory with me; by using me to carry out His will to spread the gospel. (Remember, He does not need me to complete His work; however, He honors me with the privilege of doing just that). Our purpose was clearly outlined in John 17, as Jesus prayed for each of us on the way to the Garden of Gethsemane.

This leads us to foundational truth #3, which is our position in Christ Jesus.

FOUNDATIONAL TRUTH #3: OUR POSITION IN CHRIST

Until this point in these writings, we have focused on who we are not. We are not virtuous, righteous, or deserving of anything. Yet, God chose to love us; right there in that position of unworthiness; because of His Grace, Mercy and Love. Therefore, despite our knowing our place with promise and our purpose; we might not fully embrace the depth of His Joy until we know our position in Christ Jesus. We are lifted high to be God's Blessed, Beloved,

Chosen Children, heirs of the Kingdom, servants by choice, declared Saints and Soldiers of Almighty God.

Therefore, we will next turn to Ephesians chapters 1-3; to learn of our position in Christ.

> *Blessed be the God and Father of our Lord Jesus Christ, who hath blessed us with all spiritual blessings in heavenly places in Christ* (Ephesians 1:3).

God hath blessed us with ALL spiritual blessings in Christ Jesus. Over the next few chapters, let us seek to understand our position in Christ; because, this is crucial to our knowing the fullness of life God desires for us. Therein, because our focus is upon His Glory and His plan, we find joy overflowing, abiding and steadfast; no matter what storms we face; never again to live lives of quiet desperation in this world.

CONCLUDING THOUGHT BITES

With these 3 foundations of truth, you have the keys for abiding steadfast joy for your life

In Christ, I am God's Blessed Beloved Chosen Child heir of the Kingdom; because of Grace

In Christ, I am a servant by choice; because of God's love

In Christ, I am declared a Saint; because of the cross

Effie Darlene Barba

I am a Soldier of Almighty God. Therefore, I stand firm in faith; because of His power in me

FOUNDATION #3
POSITION IN CHRIST

Effie Darlene Barba

Chapter 17:

Identity Crisis

Over the years, I had learned the foundational truths of place and of purpose, as outlined earlier in this series. Yet, because I did not fully understand the riches that are mine in Christ Jesus; I struggled with performance. In fact, I found myself at times; struggling against sin, the same sin repeatedly. Not because I defiantly shook my fists against God or truly desired the sin over God. Instead, I repeatedly believed the lies whispering in my head, rather than fully comprehend the truth of my position in Christ. I just did not know how to apply the treasures I had been given. Instead, because I did not realize my position in Christ; I was always working from my own effort, trying to please God to gain His pleasure.

Living in the premise of being a "sinner, saved by Grace" presented a definite identity crisis. As I focused on my being always a sinner. This statement, though true; takes my focus once more off Christ's redeeming work within me and focuses my thoughts on me. Because of this, when a thought toward sin would rise in my heart; I would double down on reading scripture, listening to sermons, attending church, and praying; even arguing with myself about the desires. This proved useless; because, deep in my heart lay the problem. I thought I had to earn God's love and I believed I wasn't good enough for anyone to love. Deep inside there lay a fear of rejection as well as the root of pride.

Effie Darlene Barba

FEAR OF REJECTION FROM PRIDE

Pride lays at the heart of one's fear of rejection. Sound strange? The core element of fearing rejection is pride, wanting to be better, loved more, and admired by everyone you meet. Therefore, your antennas are always alert to possible rejection. When we fear rejection by God, our mind becomes obsessed with potential failures. Working harder to gain pleasure, we fall victim to the very sins we fight against. We, like Peter scream, "God, I would never betray you!" (paraphrased from Matthew 26:3). We mean it; yet, we forgot this truth. "My power is not in my proclaiming it. My power is in Christ!"

EPHESIANS 1:3-12

Blessed be the God and Father of our Lord Jesus Christ, who hath blessed us with all spiritual blessings in heavenly places in Christ: According as he hath chosen us in him before the foundation of the world, that we should be holy and without blame before him in love: Having predestinated us unto the adoption of children by Jesus Christ to himself, according to the good pleasure of his will, To the praise of the glory of his grace, wherein he hath made us accepted in the beloved.

In whom we have redemption through his blood, the forgiveness of sins, according to the riches of his grace; Wherein he hath abounded toward us in all wisdom and prudence; Having made known unto us the mystery of his will, according to his good

pleasure which he hath purposed in himself:
That in the dispensation of the fulness of times
he might gather together in one all things in
Christ, both which are in heaven, and which
are on earth; even in him: In whom also we
have obtained an inheritance, being
predestinated according to the purpose of him
who worketh all things after the counsel of his
own will: That we should be to the praise of
his glory, who first trusted in Christ.

KNOWING MY IDENTITY IN CHRIST BY GRACE

Realizing my position in Christ as God's Chosen, Beloved Child doesn't cause me to be less concerned about sin's consequences. Instead, I serve out of love not duty. Knowing His power indwells me, I stop fighting, so He can fight for me. I have found, I sin less when I abide in Christ; allowing the full sap to rise from the roots of my faith. When I struggle to gain His pleasure, ignoring the fact that I have His pleasure; then, I choke out the nourishing sap that He desires to feed me with. Again, it is an act of pride that desires to earn His favor; rather, than to enjoy His pleasure. Trying to justify His love for me; diminishes God's glorious Grace.

Yet, we can win this war battling within our hearts and minds by knowing our identity in Christ Jesus. When we look in the mirror, we need to see who we are because of Christ Jesus living in us and giving us a new identity, filled with strength, love, grace and joy.

Effie Darlene Barba

WINNING THE SPIRITUAL WAR

Spiritual Warfare is real. Christians face demonic attack every day. Indeed, those attacks intensify whenever we are winning battles. Satan, the supreme liar and accuser of the brethren wants to destroy your testimony and mine. Paul spends the first three and one-half chapters of the letter to the Ephesians describing, in detail, the position every Christian holds in Christ. Then, Paul writes concerning characteristics of the Christian walk. Finally, he ends in Chapter 6 describing the Spiritual Battle every Christian must face. The battle is raging in the Spiritual Realm beyond our sight; however, it also rages within our minds and thoughts. The order of instruction presented by Paul in this letter was not coincidental. Before, you or I can win this Spiritual Warfare happening in our minds; we must know our position in Christ. Victory is ours; because, Jesus won that victory at Calvary.

For me, the same proved true. My salvation certainly remained secure from the moment I first accepted Christ as my Savior; however, in the day to day battles often I met defeat. I tried harder, studied intensely, pleaded forgiveness and promised that I would do better. Alas, I would advance ten steps and fall back twelve. Satan attacked relentlessly in the recesses of my mind. As the liar and accuser that he is, Satan whispered: "God can't possibly really love you after all your failures. You will never be good enough! Why do you keep writing, God won't use you to help anyone! Aha, look you failed again! Why would God Bless you? Maybe this is God's punishment; after all, that is what you deserve: NOTHING!" On and on Satan would rant, sometimes shouting in my thoughts until I would throw up my hands in defeat.

Not anymore. I have learned how to raise my fist at Satan and firmly say, "Satan, You ARE a liar! I am God's Blessed, Chosen Beloved Child. So, shut up Satan, I have work to do for my Father." My identity can never be focused on me "the sinner"; rather, my focus must be on Jesus Christ, my redeemer.

THE WAR INSIDE OUR MINDS

Spiritual warfare continues all around us--in countries, societies and internationally. We tend to see that; however, we must also recognize that there is a spiritual warfare playing out in our thoughts as well. We do face an identity crisis when we do not realize our only hope in winning this war in our own minds comes from discovering our identity in Christ Jesus.

Satan and his followers would love to destroy the gospel message, one messenger at a time. If he can destroy my testimony for Christ; Satan rejoices with as much glee as when he creates worldwide chaos by interjecting evil ideologies and religions around the world. Knowing this truth; I must learn a better strategy when engaged in spiritual warfare. This begins by taking captive my own thoughts; replacing the erroneous thoughts with God's truth.

For though we walk in the flesh, we do not war after the flesh:(For the weapons of our warfare are not carnal, but mighty through God to the pulling down of strong holds;) Casting down imaginations, and every high thing that exalteth itself against the knowledge of God, and bringing into captivity every thought to the obedience of Christ (2 Corinthians 10: 3-5).

Do you see that? Casting down, destroying all imaginary thoughts that revolt against the knowledge of God's truth. Furthermore, bringing into captivity every thought! How I think becomes crucial in this spiritual warfare. Therefore, knowing my true position (identity) in Christ, as declared in scripture; is imperative to winning the battles of life.

AS A MAN THINKETH

Proverbs 23:7 tells us that "*as a man thinketh in his heart, he is*". Yet, I do not want you to get caught up in the modernized version proclaimed by new age philosophers and the prosperity gospel preachers; because, their ideology places the power within the individual's hands. Whereas, the true positive thinking that can win the spiritual battles comes from God only.

In our moving forward to grasp this third foundational truth of position; we must never forget foundational truth #1. God IS. He is the being without whom nothing else exists. I am nothingness until my Being is found in Him. From that beginning premise; we now can move on to discovering a positive thinking founded upon the gospel truth that IN Christ I am God's redeemed, beloved, chosen, blessed Child. In Christ, I have everything I need to win the spiritual battle in my mind.

Therefore, yes; we must learn how to take captive our thoughts and to gain the victory that is ours in Christ

Jesus. Only by recognizing that this spiritual warfare begins and ends with God's might; can I become victorious over the daily battles I face.

Over the next few chapters we will delve deeply into our position in Christ Jesus; so that, you and I can gain the victory that is ours by knowing who we really are: our true identity.

CONCLUDING THOUGHT BITES

Satan wants to win the spiritual battle in your head by lies & accusations

Satan attacks my thoughts: I win by taking captive every thought, replacing it with God's truth

Knowing my position, my identity in Christ Jesus, brings victory

Effie Darlene Barba

Chapter 18:

I AM HIS BELOVED

I cannot tell you exactly when those dreaded feelings of rejection started in my heart. They go back to the very beginning of my memories. Always striving to gain love and acceptance, I became my own worst critic. Perhaps I could try to blame my childhood. After all, I was the obese little girl with a stutter as I began first grade. However, those feelings, I daresay were there before I started school and my experiences in school only enhanced them.

It is no wonder, being filled with a constant fear of rejection; that I embraced my Christian walk with those same fears. Feeling unwanted, uninvited to the usual parties or groups; I would just work really hard so God couldn't uninvite me. Although, I knew the truth of eternal salvation theologically; my heart had not fully embraced this truth. Because I so wanted to earn God's love, I fought very hard to become His Beloved. Yet, I always felt deep within myself as an unlovable failure.

Those feelings I hid well; much as I suspect you do. After all, it is human nature that pushes us to desire self-aggrandization. Yet, because we each are flawed, broken creatures; until, we are made whole by God's loving grace transforming our nothingness into Full Radiant Being in Him; we each must one day come face to face with our own inability and frailty. Even the staunches atheists such as Jean Paul Sartre and Friedrich Nietzsche came to the conclusions that life was very bleak and humanity lost in a sea of despair. From the moment, we emerge from our mother's womb we need to feel loved, to be someone's beloved. We fight for recognition, love, and acceptance. We struggle with our own identity in this world.

A FLAILING ATTEMPT TO BECOME HIS BELOVED

So, it has always been, the one lie Satan could best wield against me was my desire to be loved. He would whisper of my failures. I remember once, in first grade, having been spanked by a teacher. That drove my young heart into deep despair; so much so, that when another adult jokingly asked, "Have you ever been spanked? I said "NO!" Then, the fact of my lie plagued me for years. God must hate a liar! Yes, I knew the day and time I accepted Christ as my Savior; but that didn't ease the heart of this seven-year-old child. How could I fail God by lying?

Well, I wish I could say this lie was my worst offense against God. Instead, I fell much further. My desperate need to be loved lead me down some lonely dark paths; or so, it seemed to me. The amazing part was: No matter how dark a path I chose, God was always standing there at the end of the path to say, "I love you, Come, we have work to do!"

Remember the story of Peter's denial of Christ? Peter went back to fishing. He thought there was no way, Christ would use him. Instead, Christ came to meet Peter right at the very spot where He first had called him into discipleship. There on the shore, where Peter was fishing once more in his boat, Christ came to remind him that he was His Beloved Disciple. Never did Christ confront Peter about his denial; instead, three times He asked Peter about his love and each time, He commissioned Peter to continue in the ministry. That is the Amazing truth about Grace, in Christ; Peter was His Beloved. In Christ, I am God's Beloved. The same is true for you who have accepted Christ as your Savior. In Christ; you are His Beloved. Go back and read John 20,

Mark 13 and 14; thinking of this truth as you read. Therein, clutch tight to God's truth about your identity.

SCRIPTURES DECLARING US HIS BELOVED

beloved of the Lord, because God hath from the beginning chosen you to salvation through sanctification of the Spirit and belief of the truth: Whereunto he called you by our gospel, to the obtaining of the glory of our Lord Jesus Christ (2 Thessalonians 2:13-14).

For I am persuaded, that neither death, nor life, nor angels, nor principalities, nor powers, nor things present, nor things to come, Nor height, nor depth, nor any other creature, shall be able to separate us from the love of God, which is in Christ Jesus our Lord (Romans 8:38-39).

Not even I can separate me from the love of God in Christ Jesus. Forever, in Christ I am His Beloved. He will groom me, transform me, and prepare me to stand with Him in glory clothed with His perfect righteousness as His Beloved.

And the glory which thou gavest me I have given them; that they may be one, even as we are one: I in them, and thou in me, that they may be made perfect in one; and that the world may know that thou hast sent me, and hast loved them, as thou hast loved me (John 17:21-22).

In this last verse, Jesus declared that we are loved with the same love that God loved His own son. What a miraculous truth that is.

CONSIDER THIS

No matter how far your feet have strayed. Regardless of the lies of Satan you have believed. Nothing can separate you from the love of God. In Christ Jesus, wrapped in His Perfect Robe of Righteousness through faith; you are forever His Beloved. Believe that, cling fast to the truth of your position in Him; then, you will stand firm and strong against Satan's lies. Tear down the strongholds that hold your thoughts captive. You can tear them down by embracing this truth.

LOVING UNCONDITIONALLY AS CHRIST'S BRIDE TO BE

However long it took my heart to grasp the truth of my being God's Beloved Child, the Beloved Precious Bride to Be of Jesus Christ His Son; purchased by the shed blood of Christ on the Cross: the truth transformed me and my life! Knowing my position in Christ Jesus as His Beloved bride to be; changes my vantage point in viewing everything else in my life. Because of His Amazing Love for me; all my relationships also changed. Once I fully understand the truth of His Love, I no longer enter life needing to be loved; because, His Love is sufficient to fill my own heart to the overflowing. That frees me to love without the fears, anxieties, and demands that my own heart would otherwise have known. Because His Love fills my heart to the overflowing with Joy; I am also freed to love others unconditionally.

Beginning February 15, 2016, I shared my life story on my website, baring my soul on the pages of the world wide web. The title of that series was *In Search of Love.* Within that series I honestly and openly told the world about my failures, my sins, and my road to learning of God's wondrous love for me; because I hoped by doing so, I would help others find their identity as God's Beloved. After all, if God still loved me; I was certain, they would see He loved them with all their blemishes as well.

My journey lead me through many sorrows, heartbreaks and moments of despair; until, I learned the truth. Regardless, throughout the journey; God remained faithful in His love toward me. Never for a moment; did He stop loving me. Patiently, gently He went about the task of preparing me to become the precious bride; clothed in white that He purposed me to become in Christ Jesus.

Because He loved me so; neither, did He leave me as He found me. He loved me with perfect love, seeing who I would become in Him as His Beloved. He never let go of my flailing heart; even when, I could not see the truth.

Effie Darlene Barba

ERASING THE TAPES

Despite my accepting Christ as a young child; my mind and heart played many erroneous tapes concerning my position in Christ. Yet, God in His Wondrous Grace; set out to teach this heart the truth. In the center of it all; God wooed my heart, pursued me and loved me. For me, that took a lifetime to recognize the depths of His love toward me.

The love of God remains everlasting to each one who has chosen to accept the gospel message. If you know Jesus Christ as Your LORD and Savior; then, you are His Beloved Bride to Be, Beloved Child of God. God's promises are all true. He draws you to His side.

> *I will love them freely* (Hosea 14:4). *Yea, I have loved thee with an everlasting love: therefore, with loving kindness have I drawn thee* (Jeremiah 31:3).

UNCONDITIONALLY LOVED TO LOVE UNCONDITIONALLY

Finally, understanding my position in Christ Jesus as His Beloved Bride to Be; my heart awakens each morning with abiding, steadfast joy, just knowing Jesus Christ LOVES me. No longer do I worry about life; no matter what circumstances come. Finally, I see my future. Whatever comes in the rest of my life; I am preparing to be His Beautiful Bride. There may be a lot of work ahead; but, He will see me through to that day.

> *I am my beloved's, and his desire is toward me* (Solomon 7:10). *I am my beloved's, and my beloved is mine* (Solomon 6:3).

My Beloved has gone to prepare a place for me and He will return. Until then, I will await His return with great joy. I will read His love letters every day. Furthermore, I will arise each morning to sing to Him a love song. " My Jesus I love thee, I know thou art mine"[11]

CONCLUDING THOUGHTS

You may be trapped in that same cycle of seeking and searching for love; always feeling rejected, unwanted or failing in the relationships you most desire. Satan's lies have stolen from you the truth of your identity in Christ Jesus. If so, consider this: In Christ, you are the beloved child of God and bride to be of Jesus Christ. No matter the rags you bring, or the broken pieces from shattered relationships; God loves You: fully, completely, unconditionally. Only He can pick up all the broken pieces and from them transform your heart into one that overflows with love. No longer must you to be trapped in quiet desperation by a heart achingly needing to be loved.

Knowing that you are loved beyond measure by the Creator of the Universe; your heart and thoughts soar above every circumstance of life, rejoicing. Imagine this! Living each day so overwhelmed with love's joyous song that you skip across life's obstacles with ease.

---

[11] William R. Featherstone, "My Jesus I Love Thee, I Know Thou Art Mine (1864)," *Hymnary.org,* accessed October 22, 2017, https://hymnary.org/text/my_jesus_i_love_thee_i_know_thou _art_mi

Remember the feelings of first falling in love? That moment when the world looked so beautifully bright and happy; because, you anticipated seeing your Beloved. When your heart fully sees Jesus as Your Beloved Prince of whom you desire; you can awaken each morning with that same joyous anticipation.

CONCLUDING THOUGHT BITES

Your life overflows with joy; because, you know you are God's Beloved Child.

When You finally see yourself as the Beautiful Bride to Be of Jesus; anticipatory joy reigns.

I am my beloved's, and my beloved is mine (Solomon 6:3).

When you grasp the truth of being His Beloved, your heart overwhelmingly sings, My Jesus, I love you

As God's Beloved

How foolish I at times have been

My faltering steps and wretched sin

I searched this world in hopes to find

A love so true, so sweet and kind

I did not see the tears You shed

Or consider that for me You bled

No greater treasure could ere be mine

As Your beloved, our hearts entwined

Lord, hold me tight within Your arms

Tis there I'm safe from all life's harms

My head pressed firm upon Your chest

For just a moment let me rest

And let me gaze at Your Sweet smile

As on we walk each winding mile

My dearest love, You are my King

It is for You I must now sing

Chorus:

Oh let my joy then ever be

A song of Grace that sets men free

From all the chains that tightly bind

Or foolish pride that makes hearts blind

Thanksgiving would be greater still

Each day conformed unto Your will

A truly thankful heart be mine

When Humbly filled with Joy Divine

Effie Darlene Barba

Chapter 19:

BLESSED BEYOND MEASURE

As we stepped onto the dance floor for the mother/son dance; my heart overflowed with joy. In the background, a video of Alberto's life played; therefore, few watched us. Alberto lowered his head onto my shoulder and whispered, "Mom, thank you for always believing and always praying." Then, I whispered, "Oh, but son—this has little to do with me and everything to do with Christ". His reply, "Yes, mom; but who introduced me to Jesus? You did!"

Immediately, overwhelmed, I realized how blessed my life was. I looked across the room and saw Ron at the table with his family and saw him laughing with his infectious laugh of joy. Beside him, sat my beautiful daughter and her family.

My heart abounding with joy; because, I realized God miraculously fulfilled a promise made thirty years earlier. A promise made when I, facing a crucial crossroad, decided to stay; although, I wanted to run. God gave me the faith to trust and obey Him against all odds; and now, on this my son's wedding day, I knew He had fulfilled the promise that He would protect, guide and lead my children through whatever trial would come. The battles with Pete's bipolar disorder, with its moments of abusive violence, his subsequent death; followed by my cancer and a cascade of financial and health issues seemed to all be only stepping stones that lead me to this moment and time. Through it all, God remained faithful. Each step of the way, God gently, patiently lead my heart to know the truth: In Christ, I am blessed beyond measure.

Effie Darlene Barba

That day, on the dance floor; I was overwhelmed with joy, knowing God had done all that He had promised.

BLESSED, WHAT DOES IT MEAN?

You might wonder how I consider myself so blessed with all the trials and heartaches I faced along this journey. Perhaps, we must first define the word blessed; because, many begin with a misconception of the words. Often, we consider people blessed if they have great financial success or a life without any trials: beautiful family, no turmoil, wonderful job, and on we go with ideas of the word blessed. We find two Greek words in the Bible translated as Blessed. Μακάριος (Makarios) and εὐλογέω (Eulogeo). Μακάριος means satisfaction from experiencing the fullness of God.[12] εὐλογέω (Eulogeo) means to speak well of or show favor toward as when God speaks forth His favor toward us.[13]

Let's look at both translations so we might gain a proper understanding of the word "blessed". The first (Makarios) refers to a state of being. Happiness being found in knowing God; having found favor in Him by Grace. The Holy Spirit then dwells within the individual. Finding one's happiness and pleasure fully within the fullness of God; because, of one's state of being redeemed. This has no reference to one's

---

[12] Spiro Zodhiates, *Complete World Study Dictionary: New Testament,* (Chattanooga, TN: AMG Publishers, 1993),937.
[13] James Strong, *Strong's Exhaustive Concordance,* (Peabody MA: Hendrickson's, 2007), biblehub.org, accessed on October 22, 2017, http://biblehub.com/strongs/greek/2127.htm.

circumstances or having things. In fact, this is demonstrated fully by reading the beatitudes.

(MAKARIOS) BLESSED

> *Blessed are the poor in spirit: for theirs is the kingdom of heaven. Blessed are they that mourn: for they shall be comforted. Blessed are the meek: for they shall inherit the earth. Blessed are they which do hunger and thirst after righteousness: for they shall be filled. Blessed are the merciful: for they shall obtain mercy. Blessed are the pure in heart: for they shall see God. Blessed are the peacemakers: for they shall be called the children of God. Blessed are they which are persecuted for righteousness' sake: for theirs is the kingdom of heaven. Blessed are ye, when men shall revile you, and persecute you, and shall say all manner of evil against you falsely, for my sake. Rejoice, and be exceeding glad: for great is your reward in heaven: for so persecuted they the prophets which were before you. Matthew 5:3-11*

At first glance, not exactly what we want to consider: poor in spirit, sorrowful, meek, sinners seeking righteousness, persecuted and hated. That certainly doesn't denote the ideas of blessed in our society! Yet, the truth remains; without God's presence in our life--none of this world's blessings can satisfy our soul. Therefore, those who do not rely on this earth's pleasure; find their pleasure in God who does come to comfort them in their time of need, protect them in their persecution, and promise them His Best in their life both here and in eternity. Satisfaction and joy comes by knowing the fullness of God indwelling, filling, and guiding their every step.

Effie Darlene Barba

Consider Asia Bibi, a mother of five who sits in solitary confinement in a Pakistani prison for believing in Jesus Christ. She quietly lived her faith until one fateful day in 2009 when she was working in the fields. When the women stopped for a water break, all the women began to protest that Mrs. Bibi had contaminated all the water by having dipped her bowl in to get a drink; because, she was a Christian. They protested and demanded that she convert to Islam. Instead, she replied, "I'm not going to convert. I believe in my religion and in Jesus Christ, who died on the cross for mankind. What did your prophet Muhammed ever do to save mankind?"[14]

For that statement, she was sentenced to death with the charge being blasphemy. Seven years later, she sits in a tiny jail cell; awaiting her execution. She like Bonhoeffer knew that being filled with Jesus Christ is blessing enough. How many Christians around the world face this kind of tyranny? More than we would ever ponder to imagine. Yet, they know that the gospel message and the gift of God filling their hearts and souls is their greatest treasure. They consider themselves blessed just for knowing Jesus Christ as their Savior and Lord.

εὐλογέω (Eulogeo) Blessed

[3] Blessed be the God and Father of our Lord Jesus Christ, who hath blessed us with all spiritual blessings in heavenly places in Christ: [4] According as he hath chosen us in him before the foundation of the world, that we should be holy and without blame before

---

[14] Asia Bibi and Anne-Isabelle Tollet, *Blasphemy: A Memoir*, (Chicago, IL: Chicago Press Review, 2013), 21

him in love: [5] Having predestinated us unto the adoption of children by Jesus Christ to himself, according to the good pleasure of his will, [6] To the praise of the glory of his grace, wherein he hath made us accepted in the beloved (Ephesians 1:3-6).

There is another word interpreted as blessed in the Bible, meaning God speaks upon one His blessings, His favor. This is what we find in these verses from Ephesians. Look again at the verses. God spoke upon us His Blessing of salvation. Furthermore, He has blessed us in Christ Jesus with every spiritual blessing. Despite our unworthiness, our frailties, and our self-exalting hearts; He chose to bestow upon us the righteousness of His precious son: that we might enjoy all the blessings of the Son as children, bought and purchased by the blood of Jesus Christ. Think about this!

HOW TO MAKE THIS A REALITY IN YOUR LIFE

Knowing all this in our minds does not always guarantee that our hearts remember our blessed position; because we, on this earth, tend to look at our difficulties. Often, we fall into moments of despair, not remembering our position in Christ as possessing everything including all the spiritual blessings. Because we see our circumstances as insurmountable, we allow the weight of the world around us to fall upon our shoulders.

Blessings begin with knowing Jesus Christ as Savior and Lord. Our identity as Blessed is founded eternally in Him; therefore, our position as blessed can never be changed due to the circumstances that surround us here along this journey of life.

BELIEVING THE TRUTH, INSTEAD OF THE LIES

After great anticipation; I received the artistry for my first independently published book. This being a dream of mine to share with the world. My son worked for months on the artistry of that book; while I anxiously awaited the arrival. A tabletop book to inspire anyone who faced the sorrows of searching for love or the battles of trying to hold on to love through difficult struggles in a relationship. Particularly it was written for anyone who has lost a loved one to death or who has ever questioned God's love. The artistry nearly took my breath away when I opened the email filled with the illustrations.

Yet, suddenly; my heart became filled with fear. The steps too complicated to now go from this to the finished product. Perhaps, I am not smart enough to finish this! What is the next step? Is it worth the money I must spend to do this? Satan working overtime to cause fear and make me forget "In Christ, I am living blessed, even in a Chaotic World."

Often, we allow ourselves to become paralyzed by negative thoughts; because, we listen to Satan's lies. Certainly not a new occurrence in our modern society. King David frequently was found to "preach to himself" in the Psalms. You need only read the book of Psalms to find this occurring repeatedly. One prime example is noted in Psalm 42 & 43

> *Why art thou cast down, O my soul? and why art thou disquieted in me? hope thou in God: for I shall yet praise him for the help of his countenance. O my God, my soul is cast down*

*within me: therefore, will I remember thee
Why art thou cast down, O my soul? and why
art thou disquieted within me? hope in God:
for I shall yet praise him, who is the health of
my countenance, and my God.*

THINKING TRUTH, BREAKING DOWN LIES

Satan loves to tell us lies; reminding us of all that we aren't and can't do; because he wants us to fail. If he can paralyze us, we become ineffective in the ministry. Constantly he plants the seeds of doubt, fear, and thoughts of impossible; therefore, causing us to stumble. Ralph Waldo Emerson once said:

Sow a thought and you reap an action; sow an act and you reap a habit; sow a habit and you reap a character; sow a character and you reap a destiny.[15]

Sometimes, we reap inaction; when the thoughts are all negative based on Satan's lies; therefore, reaping a destiny of despair, instead of living blessed. In Christ, we possess everything needed to live joyful, boldly going forth to proclaim His Gospel of truth to a chaotic world so desperately in need of Him. If only we would learn to keep our eyes on Jesus.

---

[15]Ralph Waldo Emerson, "Ralph Waldo Emerson Quotes", *Goodreads.com,* assessed October 22, 2017, https://www.goodreads.com/quotes/416934-sow-a-thought-and-you-reap-an-action-sow-an

Isn't that what Paul was referring to in Philippians 3:12-14 or the writer of Hebrews as he penned Hebrews 12:2.

PSALM 84:5-12

> *Blessed is the man whose strength is in thee; in whose heart are the ways of them. Who passing through the valley of Baca make it a well; the rain also filleth the pools. They go from strength to strength, every one of them in Zion appeareth before God. O Lord God of hosts, hear my prayer: give ear, O God of Jacob. Selah. Behold, O God our shield, and look upon the face of thine anointed. For a day in thy courts is better than a thousand. I had rather be a doorkeeper in the house of my God, than to dwell in the tents of wickedness. For the Lord God is a sun and shield: The Lord will give grace and glory: no good thing will he withhold from them that walk uprightly. O Lord of hosts, blessed is the man that trusteth in thee.*

Since the truth proclaims us as Blessed because we trust in Him; then, how do we conform our thoughts to this. For me, much like David; I have found it necessary at times to preach to myself truth. It is for that reason that I developed these ten steps to living blessed which I can print out and place on my refrigerator, my desk, or even tape to my mirror as a reminder.

10 STEPS TO LIVING BLESSED IN A CHAOTIC WORLD OF LIES

stop:

1. Stop looking at the trials as burdens; but, rather see them as stepping stones to your next destination along this journey.
2. Stop focusing on the negatives and start focusing on the positive. Pick out those things that are right about your life and focus on those.
3. Stop thinking that you deserve more; because you don't. Realize the truth: every breath you breathe is a gracious act of a Gracious God who owes you nothing; but chose to give you Himself.

do:

4. Write down every smile, kind word, or kind gesture that comes your way; therefore, commanding your heart to see clearer the truth.
5. Notice the glimpses of beauty that pass your way—like a sunset, a flower, a painting or a rainbow.
6. Develop a gracious, grateful attitude in which you can say thank you to others and most importantly to say thank you to God. Be grateful that you have a glass of water to drink when you are thirsty, each morsel of food that you have, etc.
7. Read and study God's love letters to you every day; because, you will find Him there.
8. Trust in God's plan for your life. He sent His Beloved son so that He might redeem you unto Himself—what greater love could He have shown to you. So, trust His heart of love

toward you to do whatever is best to guide you to a place of perfect joy, hope and love

9. Write down every trial that you have been through in your life and on the opposite side write down the blessing that came because of that trial. Look for it—I assure you as a child of God—it is there. Ask God to reveal to you the blessing that was hidden in that trial.

10. Listen to music that inspires you and brings joy into your life by praising God. Furthermore, surround your mind with scripture, bible doctrine and worship songs. Thereby, conforming and transforming your thoughts from misery to blessed; because, of preaching truth into your heart and soul.

CONCLUDING THOUGHT BITES

Preach God's truth into your heart & soul; thereby, living blessed in Christ

In Christ, I have everything I need for living blessed

God stands firm as my strength hope joy & love; regardless of the lies Satan whispers

Chapter 20:

REDEEMED I AM

As Jesus tried to prepare His followers for His crucifixion, He proclaimed, *"Peace I leave with you, my peace I give unto you: not as the world giveth, give I unto you. Let not your heart be troubled, neither let it be afraid"* (John 14:27).

Within 24 hours, they faced the chaos of the trial and the cross. He died and then on day three arose from the grave, providing their redemption from sin. Despite that, they faced a constant barrage of anger, hate and disdain in this world; as they proclaimed the gospel of Christ! So, what kind of peace; did Christ promise us? Certainly, as He said, this was not the peace of this world; but, rather a much greater peace: a peace with God our Creator. As God's redeemed we have peace with God; a peace so much greater, and so undeserved given by Grace alone.

The true definition of redeemed is twofold according to the dictionaries. One refers to the compensation or atonement for faults, failures, bad habits, and atrocities. The second refers to the purchase of a possession previously lost. In the case of our redemption, both stand true. Before accepting Christ, we are lost. Our position with God is one of enmity and despair; as our hearts filled with sin cannot stand before a perfectly righteous God. Yet, in Christ Jesus, our position transforms into that of the redeemed. Often, in the Old Testament, God redeemed His people from the penalties of their sin. Their sin and rebellion lead to their captivity by barbarians; yet, when they cried out to God, He redeemed them. God's Grace and love redeemed His people back into favor with Him.

FINDING PEACE AS GOD'S REDEEMED

My life reflected moments of great emotional turmoil; until, I discovered the truth of my being redeemed. How deeply, I have cried in desperation, whenever I knew I failed God. Knowing I accepted Christ as my Savior, I remained entrapped by believing I still had to work to be deserving of that Grace. Yet, the truth remains: the meaning of Grace proclaims the unmerited favor of God upon someone like me. The harder I strive toward earning God's favor, the more certain has been my failure. Yet, when I learned the truth concerning my redemption; my life also transformed. Instead of striving with my own powers; I found that God's power within me, as I abide in Christ, overcomes the power of sin in my life. Not that I have arrived; but, instead God sustains me and lifts me up as His redeemed.

Peace with God fills and overflows my heart, because Christ purchased my righteousness on the Cross. God the Father looks upon the perfect infinite righteousness of the son; as the son gazes upon the perfect infinite righteousness of the Father; enwrapped by perfect love greater than anything we could imagine. That overflowing love reaches out to each one of us who have accepted this wondrous gift of redemption. Encircled by that love, clothed in His righteousness; our hearts find their peace with God, in Christ Jesus. Once I knew this truth deep within my heart and mind, peace filled my spirit and soul. No longer does despair entrap my heart for any significant time; because, I need only remind myself that I am redeemed. Never again, do I need to live a life of quiet desperation; because, I am Redeemed by the blood of the lamb. Yes, I grieve whenever I sin; yet, that grief leads me to the foot of the cross where I know I am forgiven. No longer can that grief chain me to despair and a spiraling downward fall into the abyss of failures.

SCRIPTURE CONFIRMING REDEMPTION IN CHRIST JESUS

Christ hath redeemed us from the curse of the law, being made a curse for us: for it is written, Cursed is everyone that hangeth on a tree: That the blessing of Abraham might come on the Gentiles through Jesus Christ; that we might receive the promise of the Spirit through faith (Galatians 3:13-14).

But when the fulness of the time was come, God sent forth his Son, made of a woman, made under the law, to redeem them that were under the law, that we might receive the adoption of sons. And because ye are sons, God hath sent forth the Spirit of his Son into your hearts, crying, Abba, Father (Galatians 4:4-6).

For the grace of God that bringeth salvation hath appeared to all men, teaching us that, denying ungodliness and worldly lusts, we should live soberly, righteously, and godly, in this present world; Looking for that blessed hope, and the glorious appearing of the great God and our Saviour Jesus Christ; Who gave himself for us, that he might redeem us from all iniquity, and purify unto himself a peculiar people, zealous of good works (Titus 2:11-14).

Redeemed by the blood of the innocent lamb that was slain for our iniquities.

THE GLORY OF GOD-AND THE COST OF REDEMPTION

For as much as ye know that ye were not redeemed with corruptible things, as silver and gold, from your vain conversation received by tradition from your fathers; But with the precious blood of Christ, as of a lamb without blemish and without spot: Who verily was foreordained before the foundation of the world, but was manifest in these last times for you, Who by him do believe in God, that raised him up from the dead, and gave him glory; that your faith and hope might be in God (1 Peter 1:18-21).

(They) 'fell down before the Lamb, having every one of them harps, and golden vials full of odours, which are the prayers of saints. And they sung a new song, saying, Thou art worthy to take the book, and to open the seals thereof: for thou wast slain, and hast redeemed us to God by thy blood out of every kindred, and tongue, and people, and nation; And hast made us unto our God kings and priests: and we shall reign on the earth.' (Revelations 5:8-10)

CONCLUDING THOUGHTS

The redeemed of the Lord shout amen; because, by grace we know peace with God. The enmity between God and the self-exalting heart of humanity can no longer chain us to death, destruction and hell; because, the spirit of God redeems us by faith, through the blood of Christ and restores peace between us and God. Clothed in the perfect righteousness of Christ, I can boldly go before the throne of God.

CONCLUDING THOUGHT BITES

Oh, for the grace that set me free, redeemed by the blood of the lamb

[Only cloaked in the righteousness of Christ, can my spirit have peace with God.

Oh, for sweetness of His Grace; that loved me so & covered my filthy rags

Not by the works of my guilty hands but by the Blood of Christ I am redeemed

In Christ, I am God's own Beloved

Accused, Condemned in eyes of men

Rejected, hated for my sin

No one stopped to see my heart

Cast aside some broken part

That no one cared to see inside

The scars and sorrows that abide

A heart so filled with hopes and dreams

Of meadows green and crystal streams

Lay shattered, broken cast away

With nothing good or kind to say

Chorus

Then God's Dear Grace that loved me so

Looked deep within and bid to know

Each crevice of my heart and soul

Each broken piece to then make whole

In Christ I am set free from sin

My guilt and shame all taken in

And bore upon that rugged cross

My strength to stand though all else loss

My sins all covered by His blood

In Christ, I am God's own Beloved

How quickly men's own selfish pride

Does cast away and cast aside

A fallen one—a broken heart

Who needs your hand to help them start?

Christ had come to heal the lame

To lift their guilt and take their shame

He called the sinners to His side

To know His love, in Him abide

So why do we not give our hand

To help a fallen one to stand

So, prideful man with heart so small

Be careful lest you too shall fall

Repeat Chorus

Chapter 21:

CHOSEN

The fall weather had just begun; when I first heard about all the break-ins in my neighborhood. Apparently, they would knock on the door and if no one answered, the burglars would make entrance. Even the alarm systems were no deterrent for them. Mom had almost been lured by them to go with them one day. I put in an alarm system; however, still felt the situation too dangerous; particularly when mom went to Rehab for a few months.

Finally, after studying the dogs available at one of the rescue shelters; I chose Jason. He was a Rottweiler hound mix. Off I went to the shelter. Once I arrived, the shelter tried to convince me to take a younger dog. They told me that Jason had been returned several times and was older. Before I would choose another, I asked to see Jason. They put away all the other dogs, to have no confrontations. Then, out they came with Jason. His face was scarred and his eyes looked sad; however, he turned to look eagerly at my face. After taking him for a brief walk, I returned to announce: "I choose Jason."

CHOSEN, REDEEMED, AND LOVED

I do not know how long Jason had lived confined to a cage with other dogs barking around him; but, I knew I would not be crating him. At first when we would go for a walk, Jason would pull hard; until one day, he pulled me to the ground. Suddenly, he stopped pulling, turned around to see me struggling to get up while never letting go of the leash that held him. Never again, did he pull hard against me when we walked. At first, he would turn over the trash when I wasn't home; until, he watched me fatigued at the end of the day, clean it up without a word. He stopped digging in the trash. Over the months, Jason became the best dog. Always concerned with my protection, he would sleep by my bedroom door. Whatever reason, he had been rejected so many times in his life; now he knew, he had been chosen. Despite his age, his scars, and history of bad behavior; he was chosen; and that truth, made all the difference in the world. His only desire now was to please me; because, perhaps for the first time, he was loved.

Much like Jason, God chose me. Caged within my own heart's desires far too long, God came to set me free. He knew my failures, my fears, my insecurities and all the scars from which I needed to be healed. Even before the earth was formed He knew me. He knew every time I would fail Him. Despite all that, He chose me to be His Redeemed, Beloved, and Blessed Child.

Look at Ephesians 1: 3-4

> *Blessed be the God and Father of our Lord Jesus Christ, who hath blessed us with all spiritual blessings in heavenly placed in Christ. According as he hath chosen us in Him before the foundation of the world, that we should be holy and without blame before Him in love.*

CHOSEN BY GRACE ALONE UNTO GOOD WORKS

God is much bigger than my finite brain can fully comprehend. How can it be that I am chosen before the foundation of the world; and, yet, salvation is offered to all who believe? The scripture clearly teaches that both are true at the same time. This is not an either/or doctrine as the Armenian vs the Calvinists would tell you; it is both equally true; despite my finite brain not being able to fully comprehend it now. For the sake of simplicity, one might consider; I went to the shelter and I chose Jason. Certainly, he could have refused to go with me or he could have turned against me. I could never have considered accepting Jesus Christ as my Savior if God had not chosen me and called me to, "come and follow Him." Beyond that, knowing that God is Sovereign; I know He has final authority.

Everyone who knows Jesus Christ as Savior, holds the very distinct position in Christ Jesus, as Chosen. Whether we can fully understand that or not in this lifetime; the truth remains the same. What an honor to have been chosen, for which honor I desire to please He who chose me to new life in Him.

SCRIPTURES CONFIRMING, WE ARE CHOSEN

According as he hath chosen us in him
before the foundation of the world, that we
should be holy and without blame before
him in love: Having predestinated us unto
the adoption of children by Jesus Christ to
himself, according to the good pleasure of his
will, To the praise of the glory of his grace,
wherein he hath made us accepted in the
beloved (Ephesians 1:4-6).

And we know that all things work together for good to them that love God, to them who are the called according to his purpose. For whom he did foreknow, he also did predestinate to be conformed to the image of his Son, that he might be the firstborn among many brethren. Moreover, whom he did predestinate, them he also called: and whom he called, them he also justified: and whom he justified, them he also glorified (Romans 8:28-30).

No one can come to Me unless the Father who sent Me draws him [giving him the desire to come to Me (John 6:44 AMP).

That does not diminish the truth of:

AND ALL WHO COME ARE SAVED

For God so loved the world, that he gave his only begotten Son, that whosoever believeth in him should not perish, but have everlasting life. For God sent not his Son into the world to condemn the world; but that the world through him might be saved. He that believeth on him is not condemned: but he that believeth not is condemned already,

*because he hath not believed in the name of
the only begotten Son of God. And this is the
condemnation, that light is come into the
world, and men loved darkness rather than
light, because their deeds were evil* (John 3:
16-19).

*Therefore, being justified by faith, we have
peace with God through our Lord Jesus
Christ:By whom also we have access by faith
into this grace wherein we stand, and rejoice
in hope of the glory of God* (Romans 5:1-2).

CHOSEN—A PERSONAL MYSTERY

So, let me say; much as the mystery of the cross
which I cannot fully comprehend; neither, can I fully
comprehend the mystery of being chosen before the
foundations of time. Yet, by faith; I must accept both truths,
as declared in the Word of God.

God in His perfect righteousness, holiness and
justice had every right to condemn me to hell. As He
looked down the corridor of time and saw the entirety of my
life; there would be nothing special about me to cause Him
to choose me. He would have seen a scarred, stumbling
stuttering person whose doubts, fears and desires often lead
her away down some perilous pathway away from God's
perfect will. He would have seen how often I ran after
counterfeit joys, instead of being content in Him.

Furthermore, he knew how this foolish, self-exalting heart would fight to do things her way; instead of trusting Him.

Oh, certainly; Justice would have demanded my eternal separation from Him! Despite that, God reached down from heaven and opened the eyes of a little five-year-old girl, chose her, and caused her heart to desire Him. My eyes cannot help but still fill with tears of gratitude and overwhelming joy, at the thought of it all.

VIRTUES GIVEN TO ME BECAUSE I AM CHOSEN

Knowing that I am chosen certainly forces me to look back at Calvary; recognizing that my position is Christ Jesus came by no merit of my own. However, it also, much like Jason in response to me; causes me to respond with such gratitude that my outlook on life changes. Indeed, the Bible outlines seven virtues that we have; because, we are chosen.

> *Therefore, as God's chosen people, holy and dearly loved, clothe yourselves with compassion, kindness, humility, gentleness and patience. Bear with each other and forgive one another if any of you has a grievance against someone. Forgive as the Lord forgave you. And over all these virtues put on love, which binds them all together in perfect unity* (Colossians 3:12-14 NIV).

Being chosen does not diminish my obligations to God, rather, it enhances them. Not because of the law requiring it anymore; rather, because my heart requires it from love, devotion and gratitude. Once more, I am transformed from the inside out by God to become the beautiful bride, clothed in perfect righteousness; because I am chosen.

Effie Darlene Barba

Chapter 22:

Child of Almighty God

Looking back at my life, I realize one of my greatest blessings in life was calling Charles William Garner my father. He grew up on a poor dirt farm where he plowed the fields with a pair of mules from the age of 12. He grew strong; because, of the hard labor. Attending grade school in a little one room school; where the farm boys got excused from school during the peak seasons in spring and fall, his reading skills suffered. Although he finished high school, some would consider him uneducated; because, his reading skills were limited. However, I knew better. Still today I am amazed by his wisdom. He never grumbled about how hard he worked. In fact, he would work two and three jobs to make certain he could provide all we needed. Sometimes, he would sleep less than 4 hours a day for months on end and I never heard him say, "I am tired." It seemed that for Daddy it was a joy to be able to know that we were provided for.

HONOR, INTEGRITY, AND STRENGTH

He never worried about getting himself a better truck, a nicer pair of jeans. In fact, he would wear his clothes until the holes were too big. He was never proud. Always, he was generous with a hand out to help someone less fortunate. He was a man of strength, honor and courage. I never remember a moment of fear as a child because my Daddy protected me. Although he grew up in a very prejudiced area of the country; my father honored all men, ready to lend a helping hand to anyone who needed it, as well as a hand of friendship.

Beyond that he stood for justice and what was good and pure. I don't remember every hearing my father say, "I

Love you"; but, he didn't have to. I knew how much I was loved by every action he made, every sacrifice he made, and that look of pride he had with each achievement of mine. He was a man of few words; yet, I learned so much about God through watching his life.

My father left this earth with a massive heart attack in 1993; but his spirit and his memories live on in me. One day I will see him again as we stand before our heavenly Father.

MY POSITION AS A CHILD OF GOD

Which brings me to the fact that in Christ, I am a child of God. I may not be able to always feel God's presence or hear His voice, but I know how special I am as His child because of all that He has done for me every day of my life.

> *Paul, an apostle of Jesus Christ by the will of God, to the saints which are at Ephesus, and to the faithful in Christ Jesus: Grace be to you, and peace, from God our Father, and from the Lord Jesus Christ. Blessed be the God and Father of our Lord Jesus Christ, who hath blessed us with all spiritual blessings in heavenly places in Christ: According as he hath chosen us in him before the foundation of the world, that we should be holy and without blame before him in love: Having predestinated us unto the adoption of children by Jesus Christ to himself, according to the good pleasure of his will, To the praise of the glory of his grace, wherein he hath made us accepted in the beloved* (Ephesians 1:1-6).

In Christ, I am God's redeemed, blessed, beloved, chosen child who has been declared a saint. All of this according to the good pleasure of God's will. Wow! What a blessing to call God, Father.

A FATHERS LOVE SONG

Have you considered how significant that truth really is? We wander through this journey of life with worries, trials, pains, and sorrows never stopping to ponder the truth of God's love for us. He is a Father that loves us more than we could ever imagine. He gave everything, that we might be adopted into His family. Despite knowing every detail of my life, He chose me to be His child, to protect me, to provide for me, to comfort me, and to be always present with open arms to welcome me into His presence, even during those times when I have shunned Him or ignored Him.

He knew me and loved me before I was ever born. He knew every time I would doubt him, every fear, and every tear; yet, He chose me to call me His child.

WE ARE PRINCES AND PRINCESSES IN CHRIST

Because God chose me as His Child, I am a Princess. My Father is the King of all the Galaxies—the Creator of the Universe; yet, He is ever present with me.

Even so we, when we were children, were in bondage under the elements of the world: But when the fulness of the time was come, God sent forth his Son, made of a woman, made under the law, To redeem them that were under the law, that we might receive the adoption of sons. And because ye are sons,

> *God hath sent forth the Spirit of his Son into your hearts, crying, Abba, Father. Wherefore thou art no more a servant, but a son; and if a son, then an heir of God through Christ. Howbeit then, when ye knew not God, ye did service unto them which by nature are no gods. But now, after that ye have known God, or rather are known of God, how turn ye again to the weak and beggarly elements, whereunto ye desire again to be in bondage? (Galatians 4:3-9).*

So, why do we ever waste even one moment of our life in worry, fear, or chasing futile counterfeit joys? God is there as our provider and our protector. He is the mender of our broken hearts. He holds us close to His bosom always.

THE SPIRIT CONFIRMS OUR POSITION AS CHILD

> *For all who are led by the Spirit of God are sons of God. And so we should not be like cringing, fearful slaves, but we should behave like God's very own children, adopted into the bosom of his family, and calling to him, "Father, Father." For his Holy Spirit speaks to us deep in our hearts and tells us that we really are God's children. And since we are his children, we will share his treasures—for all God gives to his Son Jesus is now ours too. But if we are to share his glory, we must also share his suffering. Yet what we suffer now is nothing compared to the glory he will give us later. (Romans 8:14-18, TLB).*

Even though trials, sorrows and suffering accompany our earthly journey, we can still know steadfast abiding joy;

because, we can trust our Heavenly Father. He knows always what is best for our lives. Thereby, He turns our trials into blessings, our weakness into strength, and our tears into joy.

Often when I am crying or fretting because of some trial; I discover God already sent the answer long before I needed it. Suddenly, then, I realize that in the trial—I was blessed in learning "How really, really Big my Daddy is and how much He loves me."

2 CORINTHIANS 1:2-4

> *²Grace be to you and peace from God our Father, and from the Lord Jesus Christ. Blessed be God, even the Father of our Lord Jesus Christ, the Father of mercies, and the God of all comfort; Who comforteth us in all our tribulation, that we may be able to comfort them which are in any trouble, by the comfort wherewith we ourselves are comforted of God.*

So, what trial are you facing today? Call out to your Heavenly Father to show you the height, the depth and the breadth of his love for you. Rest in His arms as He sings His sweet love song over you.

KNOWING THE LOVE OF GOD AS FATHER

Really knowing the love of God as my Heavenly Father should produce demonstrable virtues in my life. Since God demonstrated His love for me with such compassion and grace, why do I sometimes fear love? Why is it hard to constantly keep loving and providing for an elderly mother who has always been judgmental, trapped in her own world of negativism? I find it so easy to love my grand babies. Beyond

Effie Darlene Barba

that it is easy for me to show love and compassion to my patients at work. It is even easy for me to perform random acts of kindness to strangers.

It is a matter of the heart, you see; and, that is where mine needs to grow just a little bit bigger. The only way for that to happen is to keep my eyes focused on my heavenly Father and remind myself that in Christ, God is my Daddy. The one I can fall before unashamed with my tears, my failures, and my fears. I can lay all else aside and trust His love for me to make it all better. He will and He will fill my heart with so much of His love that my heart will grow too. That is what He has promised.

VULNERABLE IN LOVE, BECAUSE GOD IS MY FATHER

Love requires you lay your heart wide open, vulnerable, knowing at any moment it can be crushed into pieces, by injury, sorrows, or rejection. Yet, I choose to love, knowing that I am vulnerable. Never to love causes a withering of the spirit and bones which is a form of death itself.

According to John 17:26 God chose to love me with the same powerful love that He loved His son. He loved me even knowing I would break His heart repeatedly with my lack of trust, my selfish nature, and my failures. Furthermore, to love me required that His Beloved only begotten son die a cruel death on a cross to pay the price for my salvation. How great a pain God Bore, just to love me as His Child. Perfect love chose to suffer the ridicule, the pain, and rejection to bestow on me His Joy and His love.

Some say; "if He loved us that much He should just save everyone and forget about righteousness." But you see He cannot; because, He is God and He is perfect righteousness. Justice would never allow that. An unjust love would not be really love at all. Beyond that He knows that you nor I would never understand the height, the breadth, nor the depth of His love were it not for the cross. He also knows that if our heart was never broken by love, we could never understand the sacrifice and the brokenness He endured to love us. Furthermore, He knew we could not truly know His joy and His love, if we could not see all the spectrum of His Beauty and Glory. I cannot fully experience God, if I don't know all His characteristics including His righteousness, His justice, His Mercy, His omnipotence, His Sovereignty, and the list goes on into eternity.

ADOPTED AT A VERY HIGH PRICE

Did you ever consider the agonizing pain that God endured because He loved you and me? Did you ever think about how God's heart must have ripped in shreds with each blow that the whips made on his son's body? Or consider how much pain He felt as the nails were driven into the feet and hands of His Son? How agonizing it must have been to turn His head away as our sin and guilt were laid upon His Innocent Son's shoulders? He could have at any moment stopped the whole scene with one sweep of His Hand. He could have said done–I am not going to do this. Yet, He loved you and me so much that He endured that pain and Christ loved you and me so much that He willingly paid the price for you and for me. What manner of love is that?

He chose to endure the most agonizing sorrow to be able to call me His child, to lavish His love on me and to share His Eternal Joy with me. How can I ever doubt His love? Can I ever doubt His Sovereign Plan for my life, if I know He loves me? What could ever cause me to moan about my circumstances? How can I ever be worried about my heart breaking; when the comforter knows what heart break is? He who knows that to love means you must sacrifice your heart and be vulnerable is the very one who will repair my broken heart.

VIRTUES GAINED BY KNOWING GOD'S LOVE

Knowing that God is my Father should result in my having these five virtues overflowing in my life.

1. Love which can forgive anything and which so fills my heart it overflows.
2. Peace that rests in the strength of who God is.
3. Joy that causes my heart to sing even in the worst of storms.
4. Hope that allows me to see the good in every circumstance.
5. Faith that makes me fearless when trials come

THEREFORE:

Since I know that is true, why do I sometimes fear love or get so angry or hurt by mom? Why don't these virtues shine forth in my life? Oh, I can tell you exactly what happens. That happens when I forget who I am in Christ Jesus as God's Chosen, Beloved Child. A voice deep inside, laughs and says; "Love you? How could God love you? Look at you!" That is when my response to my accuser must be, "Oh, yeah I know I am not perfect. In fact, I deserve death and hell; you are right. But God chose me, to love me and to make me His Child. Take one look at the cross of Christ and tell me my Father doesn't love me. He loves me with an everlasting love and I am His Child—I will trust my Daddy today. So, Satan, go to where you belong and leave me alone."

When you do that, all the guilt, pain, and anger will melt away. God replaces it with His love, peace and joy. You see, most of our anger or sorrow does not come from what people have said or done to us; it comes from our fear that they are right. So, just like my Heavenly Father did; I choose love. I know He will be there to catch me every time I fall.

JESUS PRAYED:

> *And the glory which thou gavest me I have given them; that they may be one, even as we are one: I in them, and thou in me, that they may be made perfect in one; and that the world may know that thou hast sent me, and hast loved them, as thou hast loved me. Father, I will that they also, whom thou hast given me, be with me where I am; that they may behold my glory, which thou hast given me: for thou lovedst me before the foundation of the world. O righteous Father, the world hath not known thee: but I have known thee, and these have known that thou hast sent me. And I have declared unto them thy name, and will declare it: that the love wherewith thou hast loved me may be in them, and I in them.* (John 17:22-26).

With God as My Father; Yes, I Would

As Chosen, Redeemed, Beloved Child of God
Wherever I go, wherever I've trod
He's been there to guide each step of my way
Clutching my hand so that I can't go astray

Through moments despairing and moments of glee
His presence surrounding and covering me
Protecting and healing each wound of my heart
No matter what happened, he ne'er did depart

Whene'er I fell in the mud and the mire
As hell bent I ran after selfish desire
So gentle and patient, with eyes filled with love
He'd stretch out His hand from heaven above

How can it be after all that I'd done?

He willingly sacrificed His only son

To ransom my soul—to give me new life

Despite all the times, I gave Him such strife

Oh that I could love Him even half as I should

I'd seek and I'd savor His Will, Yes I would

I never would doubt Him, I'd never be sad

Trusting in His word, I'd always be glad

Humbly, I'd bow down to worship my King

Forever and ever His praises to sing

If only I loved Him even half as I should

I'd seek and I'd savor His will, Yes I would

Oh, precious dear Father in your presence I stand

And quietly listen for your voice command

Let the love of your heart and your Glory Divine

Pour forth to the world through these hands of mine

Effie Darlene Barba

Chapter 23:

Heir of the Kingdom

1994 was a year of horrible losses, what with the death of my dear husband, financial loss, insecurity, and even the Russian Blue Cat that Pete had given me disappeared. Finally, in late December 1994 I left Mexico to travel to Missouri to join my sons for Christmas. It would be a few more months before I could stay in Missouri. I needed to secure the land in Mexico my children had inherited. Surely the year would end soon, as I looked forward to 1995 with anticipation of better days ahead.

Pete had died in late July which had begun my incessant journeys from central Mexico to Missouri. I had taken Ronald and Alberto ahead to Missouri to stay with mom; so, they could start school on time. Yet, I had so much to finish in Mexico; from legally securing the land they had inherited from their father, selling our possessions, and moving our personal possessions back to Missouri. I had traveled those roads through Mexico as a widowed female alone driving a van and pulling a trailer back and forth, spending one month in Missouri and one month in Mexico.

FURTHER STRUGGLES

Mom wasn't emotionally handling things very well and I knew the boys needed me there as much as I could be. I just needed all the legal stuff in Mexico to end so I could stay with my sons.

On this trip in late December, I flew to Laredo because in storage was Pete's Porsche Carrera IV which he had loved. When I pulled out the car, it needed new tires and some work on the ignition; so, there I awaited the repairs. I tried to get insurance; however, I had no Texas address and no one would sell me insurance on such an expensive car. Pete had let the insurance lapse over a year prior to his death, making it impossible for me to obtain any insurance. I had to go on ahead and hope to get the insurance once I arrived in Missouri. It was late on December 22 and 2000 dollars later, when I finally pulled out of Laredo heading north.

As I neared Austin, I felt a sense of dread and fear which I tried to shake off. Something kept telling me to stop for the night. My gas tank was low and I felt a sense of panic that something bad could happen if I stopped for gas that late alone with this expensive car. I had driven back and forth through Mexico alone without fear and now I was terrified. I whispered a prayer as I pulled into the Doubletree Hotel.

LOSS UPON LOSS

Before I checked in, I questioned the clerk about their security for the garage. They assured me the night watchman was in the security booth inside the garage and that if I parked the car near the security booth it would be perfectly safe. I didn't mind paying a high price for my room, since my car would be safe. I did just that.

I parked the car beside the security booth, set the alarm and locked it tight before going in to sleep. The next morning it was gone along with my worn and weathered Bible which I had left in the front seat. The car was gone. There was no insurance to recover the losses and the police instead of showing any concern, accused me of stealing my own car. This despite my having told them I had no car insurance.

I called my brother-in-law in Mexico to tell him what had happened when he told me the market in Mexico had crashed: because President Clinton made a deal with China. All the money I had in the bank was now worth 50% of what it had been. In one day, I lost $50,000.00 and a $100,000.00 car.

WHAT MORE COULD HAPPEN

I had already lost my husband, most of what I had owned I had sold, and I was counting on the money to help me start over. Buying a plane ticket, I flew into Missouri determined to still make this a happy Christmas. I did not understand why; but, I did know that God was Sovereign and even this was part of His plan.

"The Lord gave me everything I had, and they were his to take away. Blessed be the name of the Lord" (Job 1:21 TLB).

I did not realize at the time that this was only the beginning of a journey to teach me, "Jehovah Jireh-God is my provider". Over the course of the coming years I was going to have to rely on faith and God's providential hand to guide us through.

Cancer, surgeries, illness were all yet before me. Despite all the loss, God's gracious hand was there every step of the journey to provide for us and to pave my path. He did not provide great financial riches nor extravagant luxuries. Many times, I wasn't certain how I would make it to the next pay check; but I did.

GOD'S ACT OF GRACE

In fact, my children finished college without having to support themselves. They had been through too much and had seen too much sorrow. God allowed them to be free from the responsibilities of being adults for just a little longer which was all I desired. God granted me that one request. God taught me my greatest treasure always was the privilege of sitting in His Presence. Beyond that, He blessed me with my wonderful children whom I adore, and kind, wise friends to walk along this journey with me.

Which brings me to the next important identity which is mine in Christ. I am heir of the Kingdom—joint heirs with Jesus Christ. (Romans 8:17; Ephesians 1:11) I have been given treasures beyond measure—love, joy, peace, and faith. One day, I will have a royal crown and walk on streets of gold; but, I don't think that will matter much to me. What will matter is that I will be fully in the presence of my Heavenly Father. My desire beyond that is to know that those whom I met along this journey are also there in heaven enjoying the pleasure of God's presence with me.

WHAT DOES IT MEAN TO BE AN HEIR OF GOD?

As we have looked at the identity founded and secured in Christ Jesus, we realize our position in Him as His Beloved, Blessed, Redeemed Chosen Children. As such we are heirs of the Kingdom. Does that mean that whatever financially I want is mine? Or is that a part of the prosperity idea that whatever I name becomes mine? What does being an heir to the kingdom have to do with earthly possessions? We need to go back to scripture to learn what it means to say that in Christ Jesus we are heirs of the kingdom of God and joint heirs with Christ.

ye were sealed with that holy Spirit of promise, which is the earnest of our inheritance until the redemption of the purchased possession, unto the praise of His glory (Ephesians 1:13-14).

This scripture points to the truth: when we accept Christ as our Savior, we are sealed by the Holy Spirit which is the earnest (the down payment, the security deposit) of our inheritance until the full redemption of both body and soul occur. Therefore, part of the inheritance is that we will one day be perfectly righteous; until that day we are clothed with Christ's righteousness.

THIS SPEAKS ABOUT THE INHERITANCE IN OUR FUTURE; BUT, WHAT ABOUT NOW?

God has promised He provides all that we need. He knows what we need; even when that isn't everything we want. Because God, our provider, is omniscient, omnipotent and loves us, we should not be worried about our provisions.

Galatians 3:28-29 says;

> *There is neither Jew nor Greek, there is neither bond nor free, there is neither male nor female: for ye are all one in Christ Jesus. And if ye be Christ's, then are ye Abraham's seed, and heirs according to the promise.*

In Christ Jesus, we are the immediate recipients of all of the Abrahamic promises, including our provision here on earth for our needs, descendants, blessings, and redemption by faith. Descendants, in this case, goes beyond our own children and grandchildren to include those who are in Christ because of our testimony. For Paul "his children" in Christ referred to all he introduced to Christ through his teachings. Therefore, whatever possessions we have, did not come from our own works; but by faith. According to Romans 4:13 *the promise, that he should be the heir of the world, was not to*

Abraham, or to his seed, through the law, but through the righteousness of faith.

Paul made it very clear that part of the inheritance as heirs of Christ is our freedom from the bondage of sin.

> *remember this, that if a father dies and leaves great wealth for his little son, that child is not much better off than a slave until he grows up, even though he actually owns everything his father had. He has to do what his guardians and managers tell him to until he reaches whatever age his father set. And that is the way it was with us before Christ came. We were slaves to Jewish laws and rituals, for we thought they could save us. But when the right time came, the time God decided on, he sent his Son, born of a woman, born as a Jew, to buy freedom for us who were slaves to the law so that he could adopt us as his very own sons. And because we are his sons, God has sent the Spirit of his Son into our hearts, so now we can rightly speak of God as our dear Father. Now we are no longer slaves but God's own sons. And since we are his sons, everything he has belongs to us, for that is the way God planned"* (Galatians 4:1-7 TLB).

When I think about it, our inheritance as heirs of the kingdom are both for now and the future and includes all the treasures we do receive here on earth

SEVEN REASONS TO REJOICE AS GOD'S HEIR

Certainly, God owns the world and all its possessions. However, before you, as his heir, go running out to claim that new Ferreira you've had your eye on, remember this. If you think those material items here and now are the most splendorous part of our inheritance; then, you truly are a pauper. Material possessions bring merely counterfeit pleasures that have no lasting joy and will never satisfy your heart. In fact, often material possessions here lead to poverty of the spirit; because of mankind's love of money. There are some dear Christians who may handle wealth with grace; however, most of us God saves from our own self by not tempting us with financial wealth. In fact, over the course of a few years following Pete's death, I lost everything material. Ultimately, with all the health issues, I found myself deep in debt with moments in which homeless seemed the next possibility. To which I replied, "If God places me on some street corner homeless; then, He must have a job for me to do there."

Our inheritance as God's Chosen, Redeemed, Blessed and Beloved Child in Christ is bigger and grander than anything you could ever imagine or hope for. So, what is the inheritance of Christ?

Let us look at John 17 where Christ prays to God the Father shortly before He went to the cross to purchase our inheritance. There we will find 7 items of this inheritance which Christ shares with us.

1. **Eternal life** in the presence of God. Christ prayed "Father, I ask that you *give eternal life to as many as thou hast given (me).And this is life eternal, that they might know thee the only true God, and Jesus Christ, whom thou hast sent...Father, I will that they also, whom thou hast given me, be with me where I am*" *(John 17:2-3 and 24).*

2. **Truth of God** to guide our hearts and to sanctify us. Christ's prayer continued, *"I have given unto them the words which thou gavest me; and they have received them, and have known surely that I came out from thee, and they have believed that thou didst send me....[17] Sanctify them through thy truth: thy word is truth"* (John 17: 8,17).

3. **Joy of Christ** filling my heart. Christ requested of the Father, that *"they might have my joy fulfilled in themselves"* (John 17:13).

4. **Close personal relationship** with Christ and other believers. *"That they all may be one; as thou, Father, art in me, and I in thee, that they also may be one in us"* (John 17:21).

5. **Glory of Christ** bestowed upon us. Christ continued by telling God the Father, *"the glory which thou gavest me I have given them"* (John 17:22)

6. **Redemption into Holiness** in Christ. Christ's prayer to the Father continued with, *"I in them, and thou in me, that they may be made perfect in one"* (John17:23).

7. **Love of God** poured out upon us. Christ's prayer continued by saying, God, you have *"loved them, as thou hast loved me. Father... for thou lovedst me before the foundation of the world"* (John 17:23-24)

When I recognize the value of my inheritance, I know truly I am rich. I also realize, any loss of something material here on earth is not a loss at all compared to all that I own. In fact, whatever loss that could occur here and now would be like a billionaire losing a penny. Furthermore, knowing my identity in Christ Jesus as heir of the kingdom forces my feeble eyes to see the trials that confront me here on this earth are trivial and unimportant compared to the glory that is mine in Christ Jesus.

NO ROOM TO GRUMBLE

John Newton wrote,

> *Suppose a man was going to New York to take possession of a large estate, and his [carriage] should break down a mile before he got to the city, which obliged him to walk the rest of the way; what a fool we should think him, if we saw him ringing his hands, and blubbering out all the remaining mile, "My [carriage] is broken! My [carriage] is broken!"*[16]

Whatever the loss appears as today, I have no place to grumble. Indeed, instead of murmuring and grumbling; I find that my heart is filled with hope, joy, peace and love; that is, when I focus on my identity in Christ Jesus. Knowing that God is my Father and remembering He has bestowed upon me such a rich inheritance in Christ, my heart has no choice but to rejoice. He has so richly blessed me with His presence, His love and His joy. Far beyond anything I could ever imagine or hope for He has also blessed me with family and wonderful friends as well. I have all I need and so much more.

CONCLUDING THOUGHT BITES

As heir of God's Kingdom, I have no fears; even when I lose all my worldly possessions.

My Greatest Treasure is God; therefore, if I gain nothing else but His eternal presence, I am rich indeed.

---

[16] John Newton and Richard Cecil, *Memoirs of the Rev. John Newton, in The Works of the Rev. John Newton, Vol. 1,* (Edinburgh: The Banner of Truth Trust, 1985), p. 108

Effie Darlene Barba

Chapter 24:

A Royal Servant

In Christ Jesus, our identity includes servanthood. Perhaps not the one our self-centered hearts would desire. Oh, yes; we want others to see our great acts of kindness or think of us as sacrificial loving creatures; however, God calls us and creates within us a true heart of servanthood. The identity of servant we gain because of our position in Christ includes humility, willingness to sacrifice, and a burning desire to lay aside all else to serve our King. The only way to serve in this manner comes from a heart that has learned to truly love.

For thirteen years, I served as Mom's care provider. She came to live with me when her Bipolar Disorder suddenly left her so wrought with anxiety, she could no longer live alone or provide for herself. I became her health care advocate, her provider, her teacher, and most of the time; the only one fighting for her to maintain her independence. Because she had lost the will to fight for herself, she essentially had checked out of the process and instead fought against the ideas of eating better, exercising, or doing anything to help herself.

A RELUCTANT SERVANT

Oh, I wish I could say I proved a gracious servant; but, alas much of the time I did not. Sometimes, my self-centered frustrations shone forth in irritability, jealousy, and anger. The anger raged deep inside my wretched heart; although, outwardly I went about the task of serving mom. At times when she was least capable of caring for herself, I hired

Effie Darlene Barba

caregivers to assist in her care. Then, I felt utterly demoralized as she praised them while criticizing every act of kindness I attempted. Once she even said, "You must be sick; because you are being so kind".

Yes, her bipolar disorder had left me very scarred from even my youth; and now, God asked me to be Mom's servant. Often, I felt burned out, resentful, and guilty for not loving enough. I did the task; despite my heart not always being in it.

God in His wisdom used those thirteen years to dissect my heart, to heal the wounds, and to teach me His truth of my identity as Servant of the Living God. Mom now lives in an assisted living as her health continued to deteriorate. No longer could I safely keep her at home; yet, I continue to be her advocate, her provider and her friend. Visiting her, I take her all she needs to be safe and provided for.

A TRUE SERVANTS HEART

All too often, we go about the tasks of serving others as was my case; however, without having the heart of a servant. A true servants heart, as demonstrated by Christ, is one who lays aside one's own selfish desires to attend to the needs, dreams, and desires of another. It demands that we step out of our own comfort zone to be willing to sacrifice our time, energies and love to see another reach their goals and dreams.

The only way that our eyes can open widely enough to see another's desires as more precious than our own is genuine, sacrificial, unconditional love. That kind of love we see in Christ Jesus and only in Him can we truly find that kind of love. Only in Christ Jesus can our heart learn to serve as Christ means us to do. Learning to love as Jesus loves transforms our hearts into hearts willing to serve.

EXAMPLES OF LOVE SERVING

This is certainly portrayed in a mother who pushes on to care for her infant despite having no sleep. Or again, displayed when a wife willingly endures and provides for her beloved husband; no matter what the circumstances, never considering her own desires above his. Of course, that is true of husbands who truly love and care for their wives in that same self-sacrificing manner. We applaud stories we hear of such sacrifice. Drawn to stories of sacrificial love portrayed by soldiers, police and public servants, we desire to love in such a heroic fashion. Yet, we often feel our own inadequacies or frailties at being a servant; because, we look within our hearts and see the emptiness there.

SCRIPTURES TO CONSIDER

I therefore, the prisoner of the Lord, beseech you that ye walk worthy of the vocation wherewith ye are called, With all lowliness and meekness, with longsuffering, forbearing one another in love; Endeavouring to keep the unity of the Spirit in the bond of peace (Ephesians 4:1-3).

We are to walk worthy of our position in Christ through lowliness, meekness of heart, willing to suffer for

Effie Darlene Barba

another, carrying their burdens in love. Our love must produce then actions that are genuine, fulfilled in true love.

My little children, let us not love in word, neither in tongue; but in deed and in truth (I John 3:18).

Until I discover the truth of my position in Christ Jesus as a Servant, I cannot ever hope to have a true servant's heart. So, let's look to Him, the true servant.

WHEN ROYALTY DECIDES TO BE A SERVANT, WHAT THEN?

It seems beyond our imagination when Royalty or the rich would lay aside their elite status and risk everything to serve others. Yet, precisely that is what Jesus did! He left the splendor of heaven where He remained ever in the presence of His Father, to take on human flesh that He might be the everlasting sacrifice for our sins. Jesus faced temptation in this human body. He faced ridicule, hatred, false accusations, pain, and death upon the cross; so that, we might be saved from our sinful state. Because of His willingness to become a servant, we gain the right to be called Children of God; taking part as Royal heirs of His kingdom. Because Ultimate Royalty chose to be a servant; we the guilty, forsaken sinner gain access to royalty. Think on that!

Furthermore, consider this! Since Jesus Christ chose to set aside His Royal position for a time to walk among us; how much more should we willingly, humbly serve others while awaiting our position of royalty with Him? In Christ, we already hold that position; yet, a little while we will stand within His palace before His throne; where we will behold Him face to face. Until that day, I must choose servanthood;

because, empowered by the truth of my position of royalty, no longer do I feel the victimhood of my own impoverished state. The power to live with less now or to lay aside the desires for earthly things; comes from knowing the truth and from having our hearts filled with God's unconditional, sacrificial love toward others.

LAYING ASIDE ROYALTY; BECAUSE OF KNOWING

John 13 describes both the actions and the words of Jesus as a servent. Furthermore, it describes the heart of why Jesus could do this shortly before His sacrificial death on the cross, laying aside his own agony for those whom He came to serve.

> *Jesus knowing that the Father had given all things into his hands, and that he was come from God, and went to God became a servant and washed the feet of His apostles, then asked us to follow in His example "If I then, your Lord and Master, have washed your feet; ye also ought to wash one another's feet. For I have given you an example, that ye should do as I have done to you. Verily, verily, I say unto you, the servant is not greater than his LORD"* (John 13:13-16).

Also, in Hebrews, the writer shows further how this applies to you and me.

> *Wherefore seeing we also are compassed about with so great a cloud of witnesses, let us*

lay aside every weight, and the sin which doth so easily beset us, and let us run with patience the race that is set before us, looking unto Jesus the author and finisher of our faith; who for the joy that was set before him endured the cross, despising the shame, and is set down at the right hand of the throne of God. For consider him that endured such contradiction of sinners against himself, lest ye be wearied and faint in your minds (Hebrews 12:1-3).

Did you note that? For the joy that was set before Him, Christ endured the cross; despite His hating the shame, the sin, the utter vitriol spewed upon Him by the very people He came to serve and to save. Because He knew this sacrifice provided the only hope of salvation for you and me; He chose to go to the cross in our place. The joy set before Him. What was that joy? The chance to one day embrace us in perfect, just, righteous love; while, at the same time honoring His Father.

CHOOSING TO BE A SERVANT; BECAUSE OF KNOWING

Perhaps you have gathered from reading this or my previous books, I strive to be very open, transparent and even vulnerable; so that, you might learn from even my mistakes. The difficulties, my own failures, the trials and God's victories, I try to present with open frankness. My belated husband suffered from a bipolar disorder with violent tendencies. For the first 5 years of our marriage, I lived with a victim's mentality; because, I thought somehow, I deserved the violence toward me. Perhaps a remnant of my childhood or just my own human heart and mind. I believed that perhaps I wasn't good enough, wise enough or pretty enough; therefore, I could not be loved. Furthermore, I had failed God in the past; so, perhaps, God's wrath justly allowed the abuse I endured. After sinking deeply into despair, I got up the courage to leave for a time. During the next six months, I went to therapy. Beyond the therapy, I also, spent many hours in prayer and Bible Study.

The truth of Grace I had always known in my mind; but, finally that truth began to enlighten my heart as well. Grace is and always had been God's unmerited favor toward me. His love never depended upon my getting it right. He knew my heart sought after Him; despite all my faulty failures along this journey of life. Never did His wrath demand my payment; instead, Christ already had paid the penalty for my sin. My own vain attempts to earn His love always failed; because, those attempts revealed my need for self-exaltation. Once I learned the truth of God's unconditional love for me; God, then asked the unthinkable. He sent me back to Pete with an unconditional, unrelenting love to help him. When I returned to Pete; no longer a victim, I lived each day realizing I had a mission of grace to perform. I had been sent by God Almighty.

JOY SET BEFORE ME

God used this faltering, stumbling child to exemplify His Unconditional love for Pete. Ultimately Pete accepted Christ as His Savior before His death in 1994. An eternity changed; because, God allowed me to see the truth of my position in Christ as a Servant bound by love to God and to others; while, giving me the strength to endure many trials along the way. I had a lot to still learn about this servant position as I revealed in the opening of this chapter; however, God would finish what He had begun in me. He had shown me "there is no price too great to pay for the salvation of one eternal soul"

That same truth guides my life today. More recently, there occurred a tragedy calling upon me to decide to help a child in financial need. Each paycheck, I transfer money and will until God says, "time to stop." Doing so, means I live meagerly. Occasionally, my mind wanders to desire things such as a Christian cruise, travel, eat out more, etc. However, then I remember my own greater love for my child and his family; which brings greater joy, than those other trivialities ever could. When I budget my groceries tightly, leave the thermostat turned conservatively; I do so as God's Child, heir of His Kingdom, not as a victim.

CONCLUDING THOUGHT

Knowing my true position in Christ, the counterfeit, temporary pleasures of this world become trivial compared to eternity. I choose also to serve when I continue to purchase and take my mother things at the home to hopefully add joy to her life. Every step of the way, I continue to tithe. Furthermore, I continue my writing ministry at another financial burden to myself; so that, I might tell you the wonders of faith and the gospel message.

Whatever trials present themselves in this journey; we stand strong; because, we know our position in Christ Jesus as God's Beloved, Blessed, Redeemed Child, heir of the Kingdom and Servant by choice. There are seven other things to remember as you serve and as God has called upon you to serve.

SEVEN THINGS TO REMEMBER AS YOU SERVE

1. Remember whom you serve first: God
2. Remember God promised you a seat of honor beside Christ one day
3. Remember Jesus is there to sustain you when the going gets tough
4. Remember the gifts God so graciously has provided you
5. Remember Jesus first served you
6. Remember that God continues through your service to transform your heart into one that can experience His love and His joy.
7. Remember this entire journey on earth is but a blink of the eye compared to eternity

CONCLUDING THOUGHT BITES

Because I know my position in Christ, I joyfully choose to be a Servant, regardless of cost

In Christ Jesus I am God's Beloved, Blessed, Redeemed Child, heir of the Kingdom and Servant by choice

The Sacrifices we make in this world are nothing compared to the Joy and Glory we have in Christ

Knowing my true position in Christ, my desires for the counterfeit temporary pleasures of this world fade away

There is no price too great to pay for the eternal salvation of one soul.

Chapter 25:

Declared a Saint, Who? Me?

In Christ Jesus, God declares each believer in Christ, a Saint. Well in my case, I knew my best could only be a Broken Winged Saint, despite God's declaration. Looking at my life story, how could God even consider me a Saint at all?

As I already mentioned, God called me and I accepted Christ as my Savior at age five. By the age of twelve, I was the substitute Sunday school teacher and by the age of eighteen, I was the church secretary. Somehow, I believed that God's love of me depended on my ability to perform well, earn the love of my parents, and the respect of everyone I met. Therefore, I worked very hard to please; hoping by doing so and diligently striving for God, He would truly love me and be proud to call me His child.

I gave up my certain position as valedictorian by dropping my accelerated courses to please my father who thought a girl should be a secretary. Then, I married at age sixteen to please my mother, who thought that being a wife was the only thing that could honor God. Daily she questioned me regarding whether my virtue was intact—which it was.

THEN, THE GREAT FALL

I could tell you about how miserable I became, that I worked two jobs while finishing high school and how my voice stuttered so badly at times, it was hard to distinguish my words. Beyond that, I could tell you how my husband took the money I saved for college to buy himself a motorcycle or how his uncle tried to rape me; but then, that would only be excuses for what happened next. At the hospital where I worked, there was a new respiratory therapist who noticed me. He was from California, Hispanic, and very intelligent. After months of saying no, I said yes and the affair began. I got pregnant and the weight of my sin fell upon me right before the town did.

I wanted to do what was right. I asked for a divorce to marry the father of my child. Then, within 24 hours, the whole town knew of what I had done. The church called me; and without even asking whether it was true, told me I was not to return. They said I was a bad example for all the youth. The director of nursing at the hospital called me in and said they would not allow such a scandal. She commanded, I either get an illegal abortion or resign. I resigned. Alone, rejected, condemned, and despairing at age eighteen; I was certain, God must be angry too. That sorrowed me more than everyone else's rejection. In the end, I did complete the divorce, married Miguel, and moved to Florida where my daughter was born. Then by the age of 22, I was divorced for the second time.

QUESTIONS TOO HARD TO ANSWER

How could God ever really love a failure like me? Perhaps, the church was right. Maybe, I was never saved to begin with or had lost my salvation by my "rebellious" sin. Still, could it be that they were wrong? Deep in the very core of my being, I still felt God's presence. I felt His sustaining love; although, that was hard to explain. Beyond that, I loved Him, adored Him and wanted more than anything to know Him more. There was like a soft, whispering voice in the darkest night that said, "Child, I love you."

It would take the remainder of my life to begin to understand the mystery of God's love or comprehend the truth that the scripture teaches both in the Psalms and in the works of Paul. In Christ, I am a Saint: declared as such before the foundations of the world were formed, chosen by God by His mighty works and not my own. That is one of the possessions that are mine in Christ.

GOD IS BIGGER THAN MY SIN

Read it in Ephesians Chapter 1, I Thessalonians 3, Psalms 37, Colossians 1, and nearly every book of the New Testament. We are declared saints, not by the works of our own hands; but, in Christ's completed work. Covered by His Atoning Sacrifice, I am a Saint; even, when I don't look like it. And here is a greater mystery: that truth, once written onto my heart doesn't give me license to sin more. Indeed, that knowledge grows within me until my life begins to reflect that truth.

For as long as I lived under the weight of my own defeat; the more defeated I became. The more that I understand that it is God's victory, God's glory and God's grace which sustains me, the more my love of Him grows. The more I see Him as my greatest treasure, the more my life reflects Him. There is power in knowing I am His Saint. The strength to live that life comes when I grasp hold of this truth. I cannot tell you why God would choose this fragile heart to love Him; but, He did. I cannot tell you why God would choose these stumbling feet to walk beside Him; but, He did. Certainly, I cannot tell you why He would choose these stuttering lips to sing His praise; but, He did. For that, I am indebted by love to serve Him, adore Him and praise Him. Though at times I may appear to be His Broken Winged Saint; I am a Saint in Christ Jesus. Look at these scriptures.

Effie Darlene Barba

EPHESIANS 3:12-21 (TLB)

Now we can come fearlessly right into God's presence, assured of his glad welcome when we come with Christ and trust in him.... When I think of the wisdom and scope of his plan, I fall down on my knees and pray to the Father of all the great family of God—some of them already in heaven and some down here on earth— that out of his glorious, unlimited resources he will give you the mighty inner strengthening of his Holy Spirit.

[1] And I pray that Christ will be more and more at home in your hearts, living within you as you trust in him. May your roots go down deep into the soil of God's marvelous love; and may you be able to feel and understand, as all God's children should, how long, how wide, how deep, and how high his love really is; and to experience this love for yourselves, though it is so great that you will never see the end of it or fully know or understand it. And so at last you will be filled up with God himself.

Now glory be to God, who by his mighty power at work within us is able to do far more than we would ever dare to ask or even dream of—infinitely beyond our highest prayers, desires, thoughts, or hopes. May he be given glory forever and ever through endless ages because of his master plan of salvation for the Church through Jesus Christ."

So, dear friends, where are you along this journey? A part of me would hesitate to tell you the truth of my failures for fear of rejection; but, that would mean I don't truly embrace this truth of who I am in Christ and His Sovereignty. So, I chose to tell you; because, you need to know this truth. In Christ, you may be a broken winged saint; but you are a Saint, if you know Him as your Savior. Claim that truth today.

DECLARED SAINTHOOD IN CHRIST-HELD FIRM BY GOD'S LOVE

My frankness and honesty to tell you of my own failures as a Christian are not to try to say in any way that I regard sin in my life lightly. Quite the opposite is true. I hate sin in my life. In fact, there have been times, that the shame and guilt of dishonoring God plagued me with such despair that I became paralyzed in my attempts to be a witness for Christ. After all, how could I ever point anyone toward Christ with my stumbling walk, my stuttering speech and the broken wings that would never allow this "saint" to fly?

Furthermore, over the years, I often stopped to wonder why God chose a fragile heart such as mine. It took me years of trials, bible study, listening to great theologians, and constant prayer to finally learn the secrets of how to stand firm, joyous, and victorious along this journey. It is for that reason, I urge you to lay hold of the truth of the gospel. To learn clearly your identity in Christ Jesus. Understanding correct theology will unlock the door for you, transforming your life forever from despair to joy, failure to victory, loneliness to love, fear to fearlessness, and self-loathing to a healthy self-awareness.

My Grandfather always reminded me, that though your sins be as scarlet, they are made whiter than snow by the precious blood of Jesus Christ. (based on Isaiah 1:18).

Charles Spurgeon declared it so clearly when he wrote:

> O, law, when thou demandest of me a perfect righteousness, I, being a believer, present it to thee; for through Christ Jesus faith is accounted unto me for righteousness. The righteousness of Christ is mine, for I am one with him by faith, and this is the name wherewith he shall be call "The Lord our righteousness.[17]

NO ROOM FOR MISPLACED PRIDE NOR SELF-LOATHING

By healthy self-awareness, I am not referring to misplaced pride either. A careful study in the lives of David, Peter, Solomon, Eve and most of the Bible's Patriarchs reveals that right before they succumbed to their most memorable sin they had developed a misplaced pride. That pride lead to their believing their plan better than God's plan. Neither is a healthy Christian self-esteem laden with a self-loathing, regret and the 'woe is me, I am just a sinner saved by grace' mindset.

Instead, a spiritually healthy self-esteem is recognizing that in Christ I am a Saint. My sainthood depends on His atoning work on the cross, not me; so, there is no room for pride. A truly healthy self-esteem comes from knowing that Christ won the victory, declared me to be a saint and endowed me with the power of the Holy Spirit to live the life I was destined to live. Step by step, I am being transformed into the image of Christ. It is His work in me. Understanding this

---

[17]C.H. Spurgeon, *Christ's Glorious Achievements,* (Great Britain: Christian Focus), 19

truth is paramount in you or me living this Christian life victoriously, joyously and in a way which Glorifies God.

If I am focused on my failures, my sins, and my weaknesses; I will not be able to focus on the only power that resides within me which can live this life victoriously—the Holy Spirit. In other words, if I am focused on me and my guilt; I will keep falling into the same pitfalls. It is only by recognizing who I am in Christ that I can live in a manner that honors God. The power to live victoriously comes from understanding that in Christ, I am a saint—ordained as such by God before the foundations of this world. It is not my power, but His.

PSALM 37:4-7,23,24,28,31,39,40

> Delight thyself also in the Lord: and he shall give thee the desires of thine heart. Commit thy way unto the Lord; trust also in him; and he shall bring it to pass. And he shall bring forth thy righteousness as the light, and thy judgment as the noonday. Rest in the Lord, and wait patiently for him: ...

> The steps of a good man are ordered by the Lord: and he delighteth in his way. Though he fall, he shall not be utterly cast down: for the Lord upholdeth him with his hand.... For the Lord loveth judgment, and forsaketh not his saints; they are preserved for ever... The law of God is in his heart; none of his steps shall slide... the salvation of the righteous is of the Lord: he is their strength in the time of trouble ...And the Lord shall help them, and deliver them: he shall deliver them from the wicked, and save them, because they trust in him.

PSALM 37 EXPLAINED FURTHER

Before we delve deeper into this verse I do feel I must address the two questions which might come to your mind. Some might say because the scripture came from the Old Testament, it was written before Christ. Others point out the fact that the verse begins with "Delight thyself in the Lord and then gives the commands of committing thy way as well as trusting". Are those not actions on my part?

So, to answer the first part of this question, all saving Grace in the Old Testament and all righteousness bestowed came through faith pointing forward to Christ's atoning work on the cross, which is eloquently pointed out in Hebrews 11. Remember for God, time and space are not an issue as it is for us. David's sainthood was held in Christ by faith as David awaited the coming messiah who would pay the atoning price for that salvation.

Part two of the question? Yes, delight, commit, and trust in the Lord may at first appear to be actions; yet, that is the natural outflow of faith and the true knowledge of all the spiritual riches I have secured in Christ; and not, an action of my own volition. Without Grace reaching for me first, I have no ability on my own to delight, commit or trust in the Lord. This is part of the mystery which we will not be able to fully understand until our finite human minds are set free to see God's Glory in its fullness. Our works outflow, our delight outpours as we begin to comprehend who we are in Christ and begin to comprehend the spiritual riches we have in Christ. If we strive on our own to perform, we will fall short. I can never perform of my own volition.

COLOSSIANS 1:26-29

Even the mystery which hath been hid from ages and from generations, but now is made manifest to his saints: To whom God would make known what is the riches of the glory of this mystery among the Gentiles; which is Christ in you, the hope of glory: Whom we preach, warning every man, and teaching every man in all wisdom; that we may present every man perfect in Christ Jesus: Whereunto I also labour, striving <u>according to His working,</u> which worketh in me mightily.

Paul said, "Whereunto I labor"; yet, that labor is according to His (Christ Jesus) working in Paul mightily. Not by the hands of Paul could he accomplish the work: so, it was Paul's labor; although, he could not take credit for it; because, it was Christ in him doing the labor.

I THESSALONIANS 3: 11-13

Now God himself and our Father, and our Lord Jesus Christ, direct our way unto you. And the Lord make you to increase and abound in love one toward another, and toward all men, even as we do toward you: To the end he may stablish your hearts unblameable in holiness before God, even our Father, at the coming of our Lord Jesus Christ with all his saints.

It is therefore God's power that can stabilize and establish my heart to be perfectly righteous, unblemished before God abounding in His love overflowing. Still, despite that being the truth of who I am; I will not live a life reflecting that truth until I grasp hold of it, write it with indelible ink upon my heart.

BECOMING WHOM GOD HAS DECLARED YOU TO BE

As a young Christian, I worked very hard to be pleasing to God. I so wanted to earn His love; much like Peter who boasted of his own devotion. Declaring one's love for Christ, striving to do the good and righteous things; in and of itself, doesn't represent anything bad. In fact, we should seek after that which is righteous and good. The problem arises when our self-exalting heart draws aside to pride-filled thoughts. Just as Peter declared he would NEVER betray Christ, I, too declared my devotion. Somewhat, like this: "God aren't you proud of me I would Never!" That came right before I plunged headlong into sin; while, loudly protesting all the way, I would NEVER!

Knowing our frailty to perform; then, we question: "How can God declare us to be Saints?" Because, again; God is not confined to time and space. He knows He will complete the work He began in us; regardless of how difficult that task may be.

My position in Christ as Saint can only be realized by God's Might in transforming my regenerate heart. The truth of my inability to transform myself remains true; however, by grace, God promises to transform me from the inside out. When I focus on myself; including my inabilities, I allow thoughts of self; and ultimately, pride to take reign within my mind. On the other hand, when I focus on God's work in me, transformation of my heart occurs; thereby, I become who God declares me to be rather than who I work toward being.

SAINT BY DECLARATION

When Paul began his letters to the various churches, he often wrote, "to the saints at..." Did this mean his letters were directed only to those who lived a perfect life? No! In fact, his letters, all filled with instructions on how to live as Christ followers; provide us with the framework of living out the truth of the gospel in our own lives. Their declared sainthood came because of their salvation by faith, an act of God's Grace; and not, by the works of their own hands. Yet, it remained important for them to understand this truth: In Christ Jesus, their sainthood was certain; because, *he which hath begun a good work in you will perform it until the day of Jesus Christ* (Philippians 1:6).

> *But we all, with open face beholding as in a glass the glory of the Lord, are changed into the same image from glory to glory, even as by the Spirit of the Lord.* (2 Corinthians 3:18).

The transformation occurs, one tiny glory at a time; yet, for certain, as we behold the glory of our Lord, the Spirit transforms us into the Saints that God has declared us to be. The work will not be fully completed until I stand before Christ's throne one day; however, I can gain victories, one glory at a time, by focusing on Christ's work in me.

6 STEPS TO VICTORY AS GOD'S DECLARED SAINT

Thus far in this chapter I have told you that one of the major, power-filled positions that is yours and mine "In Christ" is Saint by Declaration. Yet, we both know that our lives often do not reflect that truth. Indeed, I am certain that the harder I try to fight to prove my "righteousness" the more defeated I will become. So, how do I change that God given position into a visible reality? What are the steps to living a joyous Victorious Christian life which will bring God the Glory?

No Christian can fully live grounded in their faith unless they understand the truth that in Christ they have been declared saints and are saints—fully clothed in righteousness before the throne of God the Father; because of the atoning, finished work of Christ on the Cross.

Again, this is not a "hallelujah" then I shall live like the devil until I get to heaven; quite the opposite, this is (if you really know Christ as your Savior) God is going to complete the work of sanctification in you whatever it takes.

Every Day Be Reminded of These 4 Truths:

1. In Christ, I am righteous; because of His finished work at the cross. Romans 3:21-26
2. My position in Christ was purchased, secured, and for ever held by the power of God. It is not dependent upon my ability to perform this on my own strength. The Holy Spirit indwells me—meaning it is God's power in me that has sealed me for redemption from the moment I first believed and throughout eternity. Ephesians 1:13
3. God will finish the work of sanctification for every person who has accepted Christ as their Savior—for everyone in Christ. Philippians 1:6; Hebrews 12:1-2
4. We are not alone—the Holy Spirit indwells the heart of every believer. John 14:16-17

Based Upon These Truths:

1. Focus upon Christ and His work—we become like those whom we most love and most admire. When you focus upon Christ, His Glorious Beauty and righteousness—you will be transformed into that image (2 Corinthians 3:17)
2. Believe the promises of God—to believe them you must know them—so study His word.
3. Cast aside all that guilt and shame from yesterday—repent and rise to a new day, every morning beginning and ending in prayer.
4. When Satan, your own mind, or others try to harass you with shame, guilt or fear—point them to the cross of Christ.
5. Pray—there is no greater power than this to calm your soul than to spend time alone with God, allowing the Holy Spirit to fill your heart with so much comfort, love, hope and joy.
6. Every morning, jump out of bed and declare "Because of Christ's finished work, I am a victorious Saint and today I am going to live like it.

CONCLUDING THOUGHT BITES

Because Jesus Christ purchased my Salvation on the Cross, I am cloaked in His Righteousness

One Day I will look like Jesus; therefore, I will keep my eyes on Him.

In Christ Jesus, God has declared me a Saint. In His strength, I want to every live out the truth of who I am declared to be.

Effie Darlene Barba

Chapter 26:

New Creation

It was late in 2008 that I finally laid down the fairy tale dream that Prince Charming would come to rescue me one day. It had been my dream; the driving force that lead me down a very crooked road of broken hearts. My greatest desire: "find someone who would love me and by such validate my worth as a woman." Once again betrayed by a man, having foolishly chosen to give my heart in search of love. I was angry with God that day as I shouted, "Why must you always break my heart? Why God can't you give me this one thing? Didn't you say that if I delighted in you, you would give me the desires of my heart?"

At first, there seemed a long silence; as my anger grew—then I heard a soft whisper, "My dear child, do you not see? I have given you all of me. I died that you might have life. Never have I left your side or forsaken you. How many times have I wept for you. Oh, my dear beloved child, do you not see, every time you cried for someone else who could not love half as much as I do, you broke my heart; because you don't see, I am enough."

That day, I wept bitterly. I realized what a broken and messed up heart I have. My great thorn in the flesh, my desire to find someone who loved me. A paralyzing "need to be loved" as though my own self-worth depended upon my discovering that one thing. No accomplishment as mother, nurse practitioner, or friend could fill that gap; and Satan knew just where to stab me with his blades of lies. He knew the lie that could entrap my heart and mind; paralyzing me from performing the ministry God so richly desired for me.

CREATION BROKEN BY SIN

Looking back at that time in my life, I wonder how I could have been so wrong for so long; yet, God remains ever faithful through it all. We all have our own areas of brokenness. Each of us have our own personal thorn in the flesh. For some it may be pride, or for another it may be lust. It could be fear or anger. Yet, for certain, for each of us; there is something dark, hidden in the recesses of our hearts. An area of weakness that Satan knows too well how to attack.

We all are born with broken human hearts, dead to righteousness and in opposition to God. Hearts incapable of seeing or loving God; because, we are a creation broken by sin. Spiritually we must be born again into new life. Only in Christ Jesus can we be made new. In Christ, we are a new creation.

> *Therefore, if any person is [engrafted] in Christ (the Messiah) he is a new creation (a new creature altogether); the old [previous moral and spiritual condition] has passed away. Behold, the fresh and new has come! But all things are from God, who through Jesus Christ reconciled us to Himself [received us into favor, brought us into harmony with Himself] and gave to us the ministry of reconciliation [that by word and deed we might aim to bring others into harmony with Him]. It was God [personally present] in Christ, reconciling and restoring the world to favor with Himself, not counting up and holding against [men] their trespasses [but cancelling them], and committing to us the message of reconciliation (of the*

*restoration to favor) (2 Corinthians 5:17-19
AMP).*

WHY DO I KEEP WEARING THE OLD RAGS?

In Christ Jesus we are new creations, clothed in the righteousness of Christ Jesus. So, why do we keep reaching into the back shelves of our closet, pulling out the dirty, filthy rags and putting them on instead? Could it be that we so quickly forget our position in Christ Jesus? We feed our minds with the garbage of this world; rather than, to be filled with the riches of God. We focus on society, TV, the fads, the trends and all that surrounds us; rather than to spend time alone with God. Filling our brains with so much junk, we leave no room for God's wisdom and riches to enter our minds and hearts. We forget that we are new creations filled with the Holy Spirit to guide us. We forget that in Christ we have victory over sin.

In Christ we have new life. We are the chosen, redeemed, beloved, children of God. We need to write that truth in our hearts with indelible ink. We need to feast upon and focus upon that daily. That is power filled, positive thinking. We are filled with the power of Almighty God to live a life of victory. We need to know the truth of who we are in Christ and cling to it with all our might; while seeking and savoring Christ, with every ounce of strength in our being.

THE POWER TO OVERCOME

Too often, we underestimate who we are in Christ. We continue to struggle through this world attempting to battle in our own strength because we don't realize that we are new creatures, born into Christ's righteousness.

Growing in knowledge of who we are in Christ Jesus, all given to us by God's grace; then we become ever more aware that sin does not have dominion over us. Our old addictions are replaced by a new love and a new joy that is more powerful than the allurement of the old addiction to sin. The counterfeit joy promised by the old desires becomes replaced by the true joy found in our relationship with God. True, genuine, selfless love becomes the motivating force that provides the power to lay aside the old and truly walk forth in this newness of life.

NEW CREATION, NEW POWER, NEW LIGHT

Arise from the depression and prostration in which circumstances have kept you—rise to a new life! Shine (be radiant with the glory of the Lord), for your light has come, and the glory of the Lord has risen upon you! (Isaiah 60:1 AMP).

In Christ, we are a new creation; brought to life by the Holy Spirit uniting our spirit with Gods. We, who were dead in trespasses and sin, are given new life in Christ Jesus. Furthermore, we who were spiritually dead to the things of God, become alive in Christ. Christ was crucified on the cross to pay the penalty for our sins. When he rose from the grave as victor over sin and death, He provided the way for us to be born into this new life in Him and through Him. When we are given this new life in Christ by faith in Him, we become filled with the Holy Spirit that indwells us. Symbolically, it is as though our old sin nature has died and we are risen again into a new life with Christ; clothed with His righteousness. Never again to die spiritually! This new spiritual life is eternal.

SPIRITUAL BATTLE HERE AND NOW

Yet, while we are on this earthly journey; our old sin nature is ever present. Our spirit and soul have been redeemed and all our sins (past, present and future) have been paid; yet, as Paul so clearly writes in 2 Corinthians 5, we groan for the final redemption of this body as well. Meanwhile, we remain in this spiritual battle against sin.

You might say, that since the sin is paid for already and will not be counted against me; why fight? If I was declared a Saint already, then why worry about it? That precisely was the question Paul answered in these passages.

What shall we say, then? Shall we go on sinning so that grace may increase? By no means! We are those who have died to sin; how can we live in it any longer? ...... For we know that our old self was crucified with him so that the body ruled by sin might be done away with,[a] that we should no longer be slaves to sin—because anyone who has died has been set free from sin. Now if we died with Christ, we believe that we will also live with him. For we know that since Christ was raised from the dead, he cannot die again; death no longer has mastery over him.

The death he died, he died to sin once for all; but the life he lives, he lives to God. In the same way, count yourselves dead to sin but alive to God in Christ Jesus. Therefore, do not let sin reign in your mortal body so that you obey its evil desires. Do not offer any part of yourself to sin as an instrument of wickedness, but rather offer yourselves to God as those who have been brought from death to life; and offer every part of yourself to him as an instrument of righteousness. For sin shall no longer be your master, because you are not under the law, but under grace (Romans 6: 1-14 TLB).

NEW CREATIONS WITH NEW CLOTHES

In Christ, we are new creations, raised out of the dust and ashes of our spiritual death into new life. God breathed into Adam the breath of life. In Christ, God has breathed into us the Holy Spirit—who indwells us, guides us, and provides for us the security of His covenant promise to us. Furthermore, God has clothed us with the righteousness of Christ Jesus.

This earthly journey leaves us surrounded by all the allurements of our old addictions to self-exaltation, our allurements to counterfeit pleasures, our anger, our greed, our pride, and our sin filled nature. Too often, we cling tightly to those old garments. We don't want to release them; because, we might possibly want to wear them again. After all, those were the garments that made us feel better about ourselves. We had worn those garments to attempt to ward off the depression, lifelessness, and sorrow of our own depraved hearts.

SEARCH YOUR HEART-WHAT DO YOU REALLY BELIEVE?

It comes down to whether I really believe and trust in the promises of God. Do I really know that in Christ, this new life is an abundant life? Do I really trust in God's Sovereignty? Do I really believe that His plans for me are the best plans—

the ones that will guide me into fullness of joy? Do I see the trials of this pilgrimage journey as stepping stones to greater love, joy, hope, faith and glory? Do I truly believe that Christ won the victory over sin and death for me? Most important of all, do I really believe that God loves me with a perfect, unconditional, everlasting covenant love?

When we get dressed for the day, we choose our clothing from the closet to look our best, to be appropriate for the task at hand, and to display to the world our position in life.

If I really believe that God is Sovereign, loves me with a perfect love, and has clothed me with newness of life; then, I will adorn those new garments in response to every situation of life. I will choose those garments which best display who I am in Christ.

NEW GARMENTS FOR NEW CREATIONS

What are these new garments of this new life in Christ?

Let us turn to Colossians 3 to look at a few of the garments.

> *Clothe yourselves therefore, as God's own chosen ones (His own picked representatives), [who are] purified and holy and well-beloved [by God Himself, by putting on behavior marked by] tenderhearted pity and mercy, kind feeling, a lowly opinion of yourselves, gentle ways, [and] patience [which is tireless and long-suffering, and has the power to endure whatever comes, with good temper]. Be gentle and forbearing with one another*

and, if one has a difference (a grievance or complaint) against another, readily pardoning each other; even as the Lord has [freely] forgiven you, so must you also [forgive]. And above all these [put on] love (Colossians 3:12-14).

The 7 garments that we are instructed to clothe ourselves in are:

1. Compassion—the Spirit of Mercy.

2. Kindness

3. Humility

4. Patience

5. Gentleness

6. Forgiveness

7. Love

HOW WILL THAT LOOK DIFFERENT?

So, how do we apply this? Let's say that at work your boss has given a co-worker a raise while never noticing that you were the one responsible for the increased productivity instead of the co-worker. What would be your response wearing your old garments? What would be your response wearing the new garments of Christ's love? Or, what if your wife seems to never appreciate you while a very attractive co-worker hangs upon your every word with adoration. What would be your response if you adorn your old fleshly clothing that declares your right to being fulfilled by your partner?

What would your response be clothed in the love and compassion of Christ? Are you beginning to get the picture? When faced with any situation, we have a choice to make. We can either reach into the closet to pull out the old rags or we can adorn ourselves with the new clothing which is befitting of our new life in Christ.

Oh, did I say at the beginning of this chapter that I laid down the dream that Prince Charming would come to save me? How wrong was I! He already did and His name is Jesus, the only Prince Charming I ever needed, patiently waited for me to realize that truth.

CONCLUDING THOUGHTBITES

In Christ Jesus, I am a new creation!

Chosen by God into newness of life, I exchange my filthy rags to be adorned in gowns of white satin and pearl.

Adorned lovingly with kindness, compassion, humility and love; I shine forth as the beautiful bride of Christ I am destined to be.

Effie Darlene Barba

Chapter 27:

Enlightened with Clear Direction

Suddenly I awoke at 4 am with the excruciating abdominal pain—well I say awoke, as the night had been so filled with restlessness I am uncertain I had even slept. Scurrying toward the bathroom to begin this morning's 4-hour ordeal of severe pain, bloody diarrhea and no more sleep. Ulcerative Colitis, my constant, unwanted and uninvited companion from the summer of 1999 through September 2000, awoke me every morning like clockwork. Despite high dose steroids, constant medications, cortisone enemas, suppositories and every possible dietary restriction I could place on myself; nothing would slow it down. Every morning at 4 am, it ran a four-hour cycle of severe pain and trips to the bathroom. Furthermore, the steroids wreaked havoc on my body. My leg muscles were too weak to climb the stairs, my eyes sunk into the moon face, and a large buffalo hump grew on my upper back. Beyond all that, I now had a full beard and mustache. Sleep eluded me. Another side effect of the steroids, for which I opted to take a sleeping pill once every third night; hoping to avoid an addiction. How wonderful it was to sleep five hours on those nights; but 4 am always came with the same rude awakening of pain.

Even though I awoke every morning with pain, I did not want my children to know. So, I placed a large recliner in my very large walk-in closet with a TV tray beside it. Between my trips to the bathroom, I sat in that recliner with my Bible in my hand. Every morning, I met face to face with God in that closet. I read His Word, communed with Him, and found peace, strength, hope and joy to face the day ahead; no matter how many interruptions forced me to run to the bathroom. Oddly, even the pain seemed bearable; while I sat there in God's Presence.

I had finished my Master's in Nursing and now was working as a Nurse Practitioner; but, the debts were overwhelming and there was this monstrous disease destroying my body. Life was nearly unbearable; except, I remembered my young sons just starting into their lives. God met me there every morning in that closet to give me the strength I needed for that day and each day to come.

A DESPERATE CRY

When battling cancer, just one-year prior, I remember asking God if He was taking me home. *"I am tired, the journey has been long. Is it time to go home?"* I would ask with great heaviness of heart. Once again, with all the agony of this disease, I pleaded and asked God if He was going to take me home. Then, I would remember my children and how my sons had lost their father already; so, I would add, "please, Lord take care of them and help them to have great joy."

One morning, I heard a whispering sound, "Child, I am taking you home, one day; but, it may not be today. Keep your eyes on me. I am your comforter, I am your joy, I am your provider and I am your Father. Never forget, I love you." Suddenly, like a flash of light, I realized that He had been there in that closet with me every morning and He had a plan. He had been revealing Himself to me through His word, through the hours I had spent with Him each morning. To this day it is my habit to get up early every morning to be alone with God as I start my day. Whatever questions I have in life, I lay them at the foot of His throne as I go to sleep. Sometimes, at 2 or 3 am, I am gently awakened with a whisper of a song or a scripture wherein lies the answer. I return to sleep peaceful, knowing that God has answered me and that He has a plan: a perfect plan for my life.

Which brings us to another position we each have in Christ Jesus. In Jesus, we are also enlightened and provided with wisdom to guide us in our life.

ENLIGHTENED WITH GOD

> *To the praise of the glory of his grace, wherein he hath made us accepted in the beloved. In whom we have redemption through his blood, the forgiveness of sins, according to the riches of his grace; Wherein he hath abounded toward us in all wisdom and prudence; Having made known unto us the mystery of his will, according to his good pleasure which he hath purposed in himself:* (Ephesians 1: 6-9).

Did you catch that? He hath abounded toward us in all wisdom, making known to us the mystery of His Will, according to His good pleasure, which He hath purposed in Himself. His plan for us revealed, in love, mercy and truth. His pleasure for us.

Ultimately in September 2000 when the children were gone off to college, I went to Washington University in St. Louis, MO where they removed my colon completely and then took me off the steroids.

There would be many more obstacles to face and raging storms before me; yet, the spring, summer and fall of 2000 prepared me for the storms before me. That year, God had lead me every step of the way and He gave me the greatest gift of all: Himself. There in that closet I met with God each morning. His Joy, His love, His wisdom and His Comfort surrounded my heart through the perils of that summer. I realized, God had allowed all the pain, the scars, and the tears; knowing that my circumstances would drive me into that closet where I would find Him, above all else. He knew that it was in that closet I would find His victory and how to always see life through His eyes of love.

GOD SHINES HIS LIGHT OF KNOWLEDGE

In Christ—we are enlightened with God's wisdom so that we might know joy in Him throughout this pilgrimage journey on this earth. Look at Proverbs 2: 6-10 (TLB):

> *the Lord grants wisdom! His every word is a treasure of knowledge and understanding. He grants good sense to the godly—his saints. He is their shield, protecting them and guarding their pathway. He shows how to distinguish right from wrong, how to find the right decision every time. For wisdom and truth will enter the very center of your being, filling your life with joy.*

Indeed, a large part of our journey here is designed by God to prepare us to truly see His Wondrous Glory. Our human hearts are not capable of comprehending the magnificence of His Glory and our eyes too weak to see; until He prepares us each step of the way to see Him. He is teaching us how to revel and bathe in the overflowing fountain of God the Father's love of His Son, Jesus Christ. Step by step, He is guiding us to be able to experience the ecstatic Joy which is within the God-head. Every trial, pain, or sorrow we face holds an opportunity to know God more fully than we have ever known before. Each step along this journey as a Christian, God reaches out His Mighty Hand of love to steady us along the path. He has a plan for our good in everything.

A WHOLE NEW WORLD OF POSSIBILITIES

Our enlightenment by God begins when He first draws us to see and to desire Him. Our regenerate hearts could not turn to seek Him, were it not that graciously He opens our eyes to see Him. Furthermore, He then guides our hearts to see, desire and savor the Glory of God as portrayed in the face of Jesus Christ; drawing us into the gospel where we might be saved.

For someone born blind from birth who suddenly is given sight by a skillful surgeon's hands—that first ray of light awakens their desire to view and see more—a whole new world of possibilities opens. In that same manner God reaches down to shine that first ray of light into the dark, deadness of our blind hearts. There is where we first desire Him and recognize the magnificent beauty and treasure of Jesus Christ. With that first ray of light for each of us who accept Christ, a whole new world of possibilities opens.

Look at 2 Corinthians 4:6 *For God, who commanded the light to shine out of darkness, hath shined in our hearts, to give the light of the knowledge of the glory of God in the face of Jesus Christ."*

ONCE AWAKENED, ENLIGHTENED TO LIFE

Once awakened into a newness of life, our eyes having been opened; God begins the work of guiding our hearts and minds through every detail of our life. His desire is to enlighten us to live a life, fully alive in His Knowledge.

He has given us His word—the Bible to instruct us and He has given us the Holy Spirit to guide us, teach us, and show us a clear pathway.

> *But the Comforter, which is the Holy Ghost,*
> *whom the Father will send in my name, he*
> *shall teach you all things, and bring all things*
> *to your remembrance, whatsoever I have said*
> *unto you* (John14:26).

Does the Holy Spirit's enlightenment of our minds only deal with the spiritual aspects of our life? No!! It is the Holy Spirit who helps you with that test you are taking for school, the patient you are caring for, and even the skills for your job. That does not diminish your need to study and prepare; but, it does mean that you don't need to worry once you have prepared. Rest on the Holy Spirit to open your mind to recall what you have studied. That was my secret to being a good student, my secret to patient care, my secret to learning new skill sets for work, and my secret to figuring out how to manage a website.

Every time I began to think that it was me or I failed to seek God's help, that was when I would struggle and even fail miserably. God provides what we need to succeed in whatever task He has called us to; if, we recognize He is our source so that we seek Him.

We see this clearly outlined in: Exodus 31: 1-5 (TLB)

> *The Lord also said to Moses, "See, I have*
> *appointed Bezalel (son of Uri, and grandson*
> *of Hur, of the tribe of Judah), and have filled*
> *him with the Spirit of God, giving him great*
> *wisdom, ability, and skill in constructing the*
> *Tabernacle and everything it contains. He is*
> *highly capable as an artistic designer of objects*
> *made of gold, silver, and bronze. He is skilled,*
> *too, as a jeweler and in carving wood."*

SO, NO MORE TRIALS? NO! A CLEAR PATH THROUGH THE TRIALS

Seeking God's wisdom certainly does not eliminate my facing trials; rather, it provides me clear direction of how to maneuver the trial and keep going. Our pilgrimage journey here, on earth, is to prepare us to know Him in all His Glory one day. Here, as He removes all the counterfeit treasures to which we cling, I learn that He is my greatest treasure. Then I begin to realize the mighty work His Hands perform in me, for me, and through me. What others might see as hardships and trials I begin seeing as stepping stones to greater joy.

> *But we have this treasure in earthen vessels, that the excellency of the power may be of God, and not of us. We are troubled on every side, yet not distressed; we are perplexed, but not in despair; Persecuted, but not forsaken; cast down, but not destroyed; Always bearing about in the body the dying of the Lord Jesus, that the life also of Jesus might be made manifest in our body* (2 Corinthians 4:7-10).

I am often reminded of a poem written by Robert Browning Hamilton, I recited to myself along my journey.

> "I walked a mile with Pleasure;
> She chatted all the way;
> But left me none the wiser
> For all she had to say.
> I walked a mile with Sorrow;
> And ne'er a word said she;

> But, oh! The things I learned from her,
> When Sorrow walked with me."[18]

— <u>Robert Browning Hamilton</u>

7 Steps to Realizing God's Clear Direction

God promised His wisdom to all who seek Him with all their heart (Proverbs 2:5-7). He has promised His clear guidance along this pilgrimage journey to all who are in Christ Jesus (Proverbs 3:5-7; John 16:13). Yet, how do we know what direction to take when life brings us a fork in the road? How do I know for certain that it is God directing me to pursue a different career or to make an important decision? This is a question I am asked often by friends. In my own life, it has been a question that I have had to ask as well. I have listed for you these 7 steps to help guide you.

1. Seek God first. We see that David throughout the Psalms would long for and seek after God. Psalm 42:1 is a beautiful *illustration "As the hart panteth after the water brooks, so panteth my soul after thee, O God".* Seeking God first, is crucial to discovering His clear direction for your life; whatever, the question.

2. Ask God to reveal His Plan. *"If any of you lack wisdom, let him ask of God, that giveth to all men liberally, and upbraideth not; and it shall be given him"* (James 1:5). This is a prayer God has promised to answer.

---

[18] Robert Browning Hamilton, "Quotes by Robert Browning Hamilton", *Goodreads.com*, accessed October 24, 2017, https://www.goodreads.com/quotes/289683-i-walked-a-mile-with-pleasure-she-chatted-all-the

3. Trust in God's Plan for your life. *"Trust in the Lord with all thine heart; and lean not unto thine own understanding. In all thy ways acknowledge him, and he shall direct thy paths"* (Proverbs 3:5-6).

4. Meditate on God's Word. *"Blessed is the man that walketh not in the counsel of the ungodly, nor standeth in the way of sinners, nor sitteth in the seat of the scornful. But his delight is in the law of the Lord; and in his law doth he meditate day and night. And he shall be like a tree planted by the rivers of water, that bringeth forth his fruit in his season; his leaf also shall not wither; and whatsoever he doeth shall prosper"* (Psalm 1:1-3).

5. Wait for Him to reveal His Plan. *"For from of old no one has heard nor perceived by the ear, nor has the eye seen a God besides You, who works and shows Himself active on behalf of him who [earnestly] waits for Him"* (Isaiah 64:4 AMP).

6. Step forward boldly, confidently. Once you have done the previous steps and you feel God drawing you, step forth. Trust that He has this even when it looks scary. *"And to make all men see what is the fellowship of the mystery, which from the beginning of the world hath been hid in God, who created all things by Jesus Christ: To the intent that now unto the principalities and powers in heavenly places might be known by the church the manifold wisdom of God, according to the eternal purpose which he purposed in Christ Jesus our Lord: In whom we have boldness and access with confidence by the faith of him"* (Ephesians 3:9-12).

7. Stand firm. *"Wherefore take unto you the whole armour of God, that ye may be able to withstand in*

the evil day, and having done all, to stand" (Ephesians 6:13). Always alert and listening for His next command.

CONCLUDING THOUGHTS

Remember this, God is not going to let go of you—that is His Grace. He is the one who is holding you and has promised to complete his work in you.

> *The steps of a good man are ordered by the Lord: and he delighteth in his way. Though he fall, he shall not be utterly cast down: for the Lord upholdeth him with his hand* (Psalm 37:23-24). *Being confident of this very thing that he which hath begun a good work in you will perform it until the day of Jesus Christ:* (Philippians 1:6).

God promised that in Jesus Christ, He would provide us with all wisdom and enlightenment. Sometimes, we may not fully understand; but, we can trust His heart of Love to guide us to see Him in all His Glory and bask in His presence. Certainly, I did not know, it would be pain and suffering that would drive me into a closet; where, I would see His Face, His Love and His Joy clearly. He knew exactly what was the best plan for my life; even if, it was a closet.

CONCLUDING THOUGHT BITES

God's greatest desire and greatest gift is to fill you with the knowledge of Him, wherein lies your steadfast, abiding joy.

Wisdom is always one prayer away, God will reveal His plan in your life—just ask Him.

Abiding Steadfast Joy

An Act of Grace

As I look back over my life

Remembering the pain and strife

There were those nights of bitter tears

When I awoke heart full of fears

To stumble then to find my chair

Where I would sit alone in prayer

My Bible opened there I'd read

Of hope, of love, of all I need

Your songs of joy poured over me

Salvation's song had set me free

And suddenly I saw a light

A thought that brought such pure delight

The pain had been Your act of Grace

To Cause this heart to seek Your face

And find in You, my love, my friend

This hope and joy will never end

And now, Dear Lord I know it's true

All that I need I find in you

I leap to rise before daylight

To sit with You, my pure delight

And talk with You about each day

That I might find Your will, Your way

My Bible opened there I read

Of hope, of love, of all I need

Your songs of joy pour over me

Salvation's song has set me free

And as each day with dawning light

New trials come as is life's plight

Whatever comes it is Your Grace

Allowing me to seek Your face

I find in You, my love, my friend

This hope and joy will never end

Effie Darlene Barba

Chapter 28:

MIGHTY WARRIOR

STANDING FIRM, UNMOVEABLE IN AN ANGRY WORLD

From the horrific scenes of bombings in the streets that take so many lives to the chaos, anger and hatred rioting in our streets; we weep over the sorrows of this angry world. We wonder about the very idea of peace in a world where so many voices scream so loudly that no one hears truth. Yet, for those who know Jesus Christ as their Savior and Lord; hope arises in our hearts; because, we know our being is found in Him, our hope is anchored in His Sovereign Purposed Will for us, and our position is secured by Him as the Blessed, Beloved, Redeemed Children of God Almighty. The sorrows of this world rip at our hearts and souls; however, our hearts securely held in the palm of God's loving hand, we stand firm, unmovable in Christ.

No matter what trials we face; we can stand firmly planted upon the truths of our position in Christ. To do so, we must focus on His truth; not our temporary circumstances. Sometimes we cannot see our way. Financially living from paycheck to paycheck, struggling to make ends meet, we allow doubts to possess our minds. Fighting illness, death, pain and sorrows in an angry world obsessed with rage; we allow turmoil to enter our hearts. However, the truth of Jesus Christ rings forth power, hope; declaring our destiny in Him. When we really know our position in Christ Jesus; having already claimed our place and purpose; then, we stand strong, joyful, and hopeful in the face of every storm. Knowing that I am the Blessed, Beloved, Redeemed

Child of a Sovereign, Omnipotent God casts aside any fears, worries or doubts.

IN AN ANGRY WORLD

The world rages on, each mind holding onto their own self exalting ideologies; never taking a moment to realize the depravity of our own soul. Seeking self-glory and aggrandizement; we cannot hear the truth of our own nothingness without the one true God. Anger and violence rises proclaiming our necessity to "be justified and right". However, the true gospel message of Jesus Christ, God's only begotten son; remains a message of humility, love, and kindness. Even within the ranks of the churches, too often; we fail to present His truth as we want to force our thoughts upon others. Instead, our mission should remain one of presenting Christ to the world; allowing the transforming work of the Holy Spirit to then change the hearts of stone into hearts of truth and kindness.

Evil exists in the world and dominates at times. Throughout history there remains the remnants of wars. This truth remains a part of Old Testament history; when, yes God sends forth armies to battle against idolatry, hate, and evil. So, please do not misunderstand me by thinking I oppose those whom God calls to protect us. Laws remain necessary; for humanity cannot survive without laws to govern our depraved hearts and borders to protect us; because, yes, evil exists and runs rampant upon this earth for now, until God calls forth His Final Judgement. What I am saying: those who trust in God can rise above the noise of an angry world, individually maintaining their hope, love and strength because they know their position in Christ Jesus. When we forget this, even for a moment; anger and despair invades our own heart. Anger should have no place in the heart of a Christian; yet, too often we allow it in.

HOW TO STAND FIRM, UNMOVEABLE

Jesus told us:

These things I have spoken unto you, that in me ye might have peace. In the world ye shall have tribulation: but be of good cheer; I have overcome the world (John 16:33).

Our peace does not depend upon this world; because we find our peace with God. Because of Jesus Christ having paid our penalty at Calvary, we through faith are redeemed when we accept the truth of the gospel. At peace with God, our hearts can rest from the turmoil we faced. With God on our side, we can trust Him with our life; no matter what trials come our way. Furthermore,

Paul, an apostle of Jesus Christ by the will of God, to the saints which are at Ephesus, and to the faithful in Christ Jesus: Grace be to you, and peace, from God our Father, and from the Lord Jesus Christ. Blessed be the God and Father of our Lord Jesus Christ, who hath blessed us with all spiritual blessings in heavenly places in Christ: According as he hath chosen us in him before the foundation of the world, that we should be holy and without blame before him in love: Having predestinated us unto the adoption of children by Jesus Christ to himself, according to the good pleasure of his will. To the praise of the glory of his grace, wherein he hath made us accepted in the beloved (Ephesians 1:1-6).

KNOWING OUR POSITION BRINGS PEACE, JOY AND HOPE-NO MATTER WHAT

When we begin to fully understand our position in Christ Jesus as God's Beloved, Blessed, Redeemed Child; heir of the Kingdom; what is left to ever worry about? In Christ Jesus, we possess every spiritual blessing in heavenly places. What more could we ever want.? We must spend time alone with God, searching the scripture and preparing to face this world by prayer within our own private war room. We do live in an angry world where evil runs rampant; however, our war room prepares us to face the world through personal devotion to God in prayer and Bible study. There, we discover our position in Christ as mighty warriors of truth, love, peace, and joy. Then, we become victorious over life's problems; which can never take us down.

PUTTING ON THE ARMOR OF GOD

Paul tells us to put on the whole armor of God.

Finally, my brethren, be strong in the Lord, and in the power of his might. Put on the whole armour of God, that ye may be able to stand against the wiles of the devil. For we wrestle not against flesh and blood, but against principalities, against powers, against the rulers of the darkness of this world, against spiritual wickedness in high places. Wherefore take unto you the whole armour of God, that ye may be able to withstand in the evil day, and having done all, to stand. Stand therefore, having your loins girt about with truth, and having on the breastplate of righteousness; And your feet shod with the preparation of the gospel of peace; Above all, taking the shield of faith, wherewith ye shall be able to quench all the fiery darts of the wicked. And take the helmet of salvation, and the sword of the Spirit, which is the word of God: Praying always with all prayer and supplication in the Spirit, and watching thereunto with all perseverance and supplication for all saints (Ephesians 6:10-18).

THE WAR ROOM PREPARES US FOR BATTLE

We face battles from every side; including, those battles within our own hearts. Yet, these battles; even those wars among nations; are being waged in a higher realm than we can imagine. We battle against principalities, powers, rulers of darkness, and spiritual wickedness in high places.

Daniel 10 gives us a glimpse into the spiritual warfare surrounding us and our world. Gabriel was temporarily detained in delivering God's message to Daniel while battling

~ 217~

demons; until, the Archangel Michael assisted him in battle. Don't think for a minute that God's host of angels could ever lose the battle. They already have the full victory; yet, for now the warfare rages on for a moment in time. This is due to God's grace extending His hand to one more sinner, bidding them to come and drink from His fountain of life.

Knowing that the battles are being fought on a spiritual plane, we must engage as mighty warriors; through spiritual means. Note the pieces of our armor: truth, righteousness, faith, peace, and salvation. Our feet shod with the gospel message, an urgency to spread the gospel. What are our weapons, they are the Word of God-wielded by the Holy Spirit and Prayer? We cannot ever hope to face the battles of each day, the battles within our nation, or those around the world without knowing the battle begins in our war room alone with God on our knees with our Bible opened before us.

CONSIDER THIS

Whenever you are joyous, praising God, and begin your day with great hope. Suddenly, someone says something or your boss speaks down to you with utter disrespect or you suddenly have a thought of fear enter your mind. Anger, fear, feelings of inadequacy, and sadness begins to overtake your thoughts until you can no longer feel trust. Indeed, that is an example of Satanic Spirits which we must fight each day. They come whispering to us the lies that "god really is not good, nor does he want good for us, or god does not love us." There are also evil spirits of corruption, lies, and pride that override governments, news media, and nations.

Even those battles surrounding us within our nation and around the world. The battles against ISIS, the evil forces in North Korea, and even the war on drugs. None of this can be won unless God people go to battle first within their individual war rooms; where, God steps in to develop the plan of action.

ANOTHER EXAMPLE: DANIEL.

Daniel had become overwhelmed by despair to the point that he did not bathe, eat, nor drink anything. This great hero of faith had fallen into a deep depression as he realized that wars, violence, terrors, tragedies, and sin would continue to ravage the world for many years to come. He had lost sight of the truth that God would send a Savior to redeem all who would believe. He had lost sight that God would win the victory. It is so easy to lose sight of the goodness of God when we are in the heat of the battle.

As Daniel was spiraling downward in despair; having prayed until he could no longer. He thought his prayers were going unheard and unanswered. Ever been there? That is when Gabriel arrived.

And he said unto me, O Daniel, a man greatly beloved, understand the words that I speak unto thee, and stand upright: for unto thee am I now sent. And when he had spoken this word unto me, I stood trembling. Then said he unto me, Fear not, Daniel: for from the first day that thou didst set thine heart to understand, and to chasten thyself before thy

God, thy words were heard, and I am come
for thy words (Daniel 10:11-12).

Our prayers are heard and God sends forth His angels to respond immediately. Sometimes because of all the spiritual warfare around us, it may feel to us that the prayers are delayed. But we can be certain, they are being heard and answered immediately! It may take time for the preparation of everything else; but, the answer is already on the way. This was the case in Daniel 10. The messenger angel tells Daniel that he had been delayed while battling demoniac spirits which had been assigned to regions of the world. To answer Daniel's prayer for the nation of Israel, God was making the pathway clear in all the regions of the other nations.

Prior to Jesus sending the Holy Spirit to indwell every person who accepts Christ as Savior, it was necessary for God to send messengers to His people. We have the Holy Spirit indwelling us to assist us in every battle we face. We must be preparing for each day to face those battles and we must be in that war room, praying for our nation; and the world.

THE BATTLES RAGE ON

We might wonder why God has not come to end all war. Look at the war-torn nations in the middle east. We groan at the atrocities, failing to see that the fastest growing Christian churches are there. Within the ravages, God is calling people to Himself. Can we question God? People are being saved. Their eternity matters more to God than the moments.

Hath not the potter power over the clay, of
the same lump to make one vessel unto

honour, and another unto dishonour? What
if God, willing to shew his wrath, and to make
his power known, endured with much
longsuffering the vessels of wrath fitted to
destruction: And that he might make known
the riches of his glory on the vessels of
mercy, which he had afore prepared unto
glory (Romans 9:21-23).

FINAL THOUGHTS

In Christ Jesus, we are Mighty Warriors. As such, we must prepare for the battle by putting the armor of God. We do that through spending time alone with God, studying His word and communing with Him in prayer.

The greatest battle we fight needs to be for the lost. We are to always have our feet shod with the preparation of the gospel message to carry it to all whom we meet.

Last week, Mom was in a battle. She has fought many years against her bipolar disorder. During her battle last week against despair, I went into battle with fasting prayer for her. For the first time in my life, she is happy, even joyful; resting in God. What a miraculous battle won! I had prayed before; but, never with such fervor.

Effie Darlene Barba

Chapter 29:

Gifted, God Endowed

Over the years, I found myself running in circles; attempting to be everything for everybody. Motivated by a need to be loved, I worked day and night. Often, afraid to ask for help; I believed I must stand alone; while giving to others. As such, I found myself feeling drained; because, I had nothing left to give. Or so, I believed. Furthermore, I found myself working so hard to perform for God, that I despaired with each "failure"-real or perceived. Always motivated by the fear of rejection, I remained vulnerable to Satan's whispering lies. "You will never be good enough! Look, you just fell again into the same sin. What kind of fool are you?" Then, one day; listening to Charles Stanley; I heard him preaching about the spiritual gift of Mercy. Every word He spoke, pulled at my heart, revealing to me the truth of my personal struggle.

I hurried to the Intouch.org website to listen to the full series. Furthermore, I keep a CD copy of the series on my shelf, always. I pull it out and listen to it again; whenever, I find myself growing selfish, cranky and tired of ministry. Those symptoms are the first telltale sign that "Mercy" is out of step with God. How quickly I forget who I am in Christ, needing a reminder! In fact, this past weekend; I found myself struggling. Frustrated with me, I wanted to withdraw into a cocoon. The difference between now and 15 years ago? Now, I recognize the signs quickly, knowing where to turn. Therefore, never to be bound in a life of quiet desperation; because, the Holy Spirit guides me back to that place and time where I first knew, in Christ Jesus, I have victory over my despair.

ONE BODY WITH MANY PARTS

Jesus Christ portrays the perfect embodiment of all the spiritual gifts flowing forth in one person. However, in the body of His Church, the gifts are uniquely given so that everyone holds one primary motivational gift with some holding a secondary motivational gift. No one stands completely alone holding all the gifts, apart from Jesus. Purposely, God divided the gifts, so none of us could stand as an island alone. Look at this verse:

> *Endeavoring to keep the unity of the Spirit in the bond of peace. There is one body, and one Spirit, even as ye are called in one hope of your calling; [5] One Lord, one faith, one baptism, One God and Father of all, who is above all, and through all, and in you all. But unto every one of us is given grace according to the measure of the gift of Christ. Wherefore he saith, "When he ascended up on high, he led captivity captive, and gave gifts unto men"* (Ephesians 4:3-7).

Note Paul said, "But unto every one of us is given grace according to the measure of THE GIFT of Christ" Christ bestowed upon each of us who accept Him as Lord and King, one primary Spiritual gift of motivation; rather than all seven. Although, there are some I have seen who display two: (a primary with a minor) which either complement each other or contrast for balance. To fully understand the body of the church, each member must learn their own function and purpose within the body. These were given in this manner to keep the unity of the Spirit in a bond of peace. We are not to stand as an island in this journey on earth.

UNIQUELY INTERTWINED

The hand as it plunges itself into the fire; cannot tell the brain, "Withdraw me from the fire." Quite the opposite occurs. The hand reports to the brain "I hurt". Thus, the brain tells the hand to withdraw itself from the flame. Each body part has its own unique function; however, they must harmoniously work together to function to their fullest potential.

Each of us must understand the intricacies of our own motivational gift; how it complements another's gift, and how they all inter-work to a perfect harmony.

Spiritual Gift Analysis: 7 Unique gifts of Motivation

For I say, through the grace given unto me, to every man that is among you, not to think of himself more highly than he ought to think; but to think soberly, according as God hath dealt to every man the measure of faith. For as we have many members in one body, and all members have not the same office: So, we, being many, are one body in Christ, and everyone members one of another. Having then gifts differing according to the grace that is given to us, whether prophecy, let us prophesy according to the proportion of faith; Or ministry, let us wait on our ministering: or he that teacheth, on teaching; Or he that exhorteth, on exhortation: he that giveth, let him do it with simplicity; he that ruleth, with diligence; he that sheweth mercy, with cheerfulness. Let love be without dissimulation (Romans 12: 3-9).

So, the 7 Motivational Spiritual gifts that we will be exploring in this chapter are:

1. Leadership (Organization)
2. Service (Ministry)
3. Mercy
4. Giving (Money Management)
5. Exhortation
6. Teacher
7. Prophesy (Justice)

With each gift, we will explore its unique role in the body of the church. What it looks like when we are truly walking in the spirit. What it looks like when we are walking in the flesh. We need to learn how each motivational gift interacts with other Christian's spiritual gift to fully function as the body of Christ's Church. Furthermore, we need to know the pitfalls we must be looking out for. Nearly everything I have learned about spiritual gifts, I must attribute to Charles Stanley and his CD series, *God's Children Gifted for Ministry.*[19]

CONSIDERING THIS

As we do this, try to identify your own primary spiritual gift. Think about other people you have meet in this

---

[19] Charles Stanley, "God's Children Gifted for Ministry", *Intouch.org.,* accessed October 26,2017, https://store.intouch.org/p-2654-gods-children-gifted-for-ministry.aspx

journey and try to identify their primary motivational gift. Together, we form a fully functional body of Christ's Church knit together by love.

Knowledge of our individual motivational gifts combined with application of that knowledge leads to harmony-both personal and interpersonal. Furthermore, beyond simply acknowledging our own motivational gift; we need to understand each gifts purpose, strengths, and pitfalls. We must be sensitive to how another's motivational gift affects their perception of every situation; in contrast to our own. Furthermore, we need to be keenly aware of how our words and actions affect those around us, depending on their perspective. So, let us embark into a study of the various spiritual gifts; beginning with Leadership.

Before we discuss leadership: I do think it is important to review a few facts. In Christ Jesus, we are each given specific motivational gifts to assist in the furtherance of the church. Together we continue the work of spreading the gospel of Jesus Christ to a world in need. We do this by harmoniously joining hands, celebrating each other's gifts with compassion, empathy and love. We need to humbly seek to lift each other up.

Even so ye, forasmuch as ye are zealous of spiritual gifts, seek that ye may excel to the edifying of the church (1 Corinthians 14:12).

We are to join hands with others who have varying gifts that we might further edify the church. To do that in love we must learn about each of the gifts; because, only through knowledge can we understand each other.

LEADERSHIP (THE GIFT OF ORGANIZATION)

Those given the gift of leadership uniquely can see every project in its completed form. With clarity, they break down the steps needed to reach the goal. Recognizing the resources around them, they create a well-organized master plan. Realizing that they don't need to perform every step; those gifted as leaders evaluate their resources. Assigning the best person for each task, the leader clearly sees other's talents. Possessing loyalty, those with the gift of leadership demand loyalty in return. They quickly reject those who appear to have betrayed them. These leaders don't want to hear any negativity; because, they clearly see the finished product. Neither do they have patience for hesitation or doubt. They emotionally detach themselves from the details, to keep the big picture in mind. Having outlined the process, they focus on the final product. They do not crumble in the face of criticism.

Misunderstood because of their intolerance of negativity; the leader is criticized as being insensitive. Those with the gift of leadership don't want to hear about another's excuses or frustration; because, the leader, himself or herself brushes aside their own emotions to focus on the goal. Therefore, they are often seen as cold and uncaring. While the truth is they do care. They know that completing the task brings security, peace and joy to everyone.

We need leaders in the church; otherwise, things would get stuck in unending committees, never going anywhere. So, let us open our hearts to embrace the beauty of their gift; instead, of pushing them into solitude.

Biblical Example of Leadership: Lydia

And a certain woman named Lydia, a seller of purple, of the city of Thyatira, which worshipped God, heard us: whose heart the Lord opened, that she attended unto the things which were spoken of Paul. And when she was baptized, and her household, she besought us, saying, If ye have judged me to be faithful to the Lord, come into my house, and abide there. And she constrained us (Acts 16:14-15).

She was a business woman: organized, persuasive, with a plan; which she carried out through skill and determination.

Later in the same chapter, it was Lydia's house where Paul and Silas went when they were released from prison.

The Leader: In the Spirit Vs in The Flesh

When walking in the spirit those with the gift of leadership demonstrate: orderliness, initiative (self-starters), responsibility, humility, decisiveness, determination and loyalty. In contrast, when they act out of the flesh; they become disorganized, apathetic, unreliable, prideful, indecisive, fainthearted and unfaithful.[20]

---

[20] Stanley, "Gifted," Part 7 Organization

Effie Darlene Barba

Do You Know Someone Who Is a Leader?

Think of people in your family, your church, your job, your inner circle of friends, and your community. Try to recognize people with this motivational gift. Once identified, try to be sensitive to their aversion for negativity. Don't be offended when they cannot listen to your woes and sorrows. Garner from their strengths; turning to them when you need to see the bigger picture. When the leader chooses you to perform a task; remember, they think you are the best. So, see it as an honor.

If Leadership Is Your Motivational Gift

If you identify this as your motivational gift, ask God for the patience to deal with those who cannot see the big picture. Learn gentleness and kindness, leading the group with love. Thank God for your gift. Practice patience toward those less organized. When people need to pour out their hearts, listen at least long enough to determine who might be able to help them. Perhaps, you can refer them to others whose spiritual gifts will best help them. After all, you are best suited to identify who can accomplish that task. Keep in mind your greatest goal: spreading the gospel of Christ to all the world.

Paul's Admonition: to those with this gift: "he who leads, with diligence" (Romans 12:8). Perhaps of all the gifts, the leader most needs diligence to persist no matter what obstacles present themselves along the way. The leader must always keep focus and never lose sight of the goal; regardless of the obstacles that present themselves along the way.

THE GIFT OF MINISTRY (SERVICE)

Those gifted with Service (or otherwise known as Ministry) as their primary motivation play a vital role in the furtherance of the church. Uniquely, they see clearly the needs of others around them and cannot be content until those needs are met. Deriving their joy from seeing the need fulfilled, they jump quickly into action and continue until the task is complete. Because they intently desire to know they really fulfilled the needs, they need to hear "Thank you". This need for a "Thank you" is not born out of pride or selfish desire; instead, it comes from a deep concern over the one they are trying to help. Often, the person gifted with Service as their motivational gift; fear their task is not done. Perhaps they should have done more! To them, failure is not an option.

Misunderstood because of their boldness to jump into another's situation, they are criticized for being too eager. Think about the women at a church dinner who arrives early, sets up all the tables and chairs, constantly asking where they can help and then stays until the last person served and dish washed. People without the gift of service, see those with as "grand-standing"; failing to appreciate their nature is such. They really aren't trying to steal the show. Truly, they want to serve and can't be satisfied until they have fulfilled all the needs in front of them. When, those with the gift of service feel their acts of service are unappreciated; they withdraw into feelings of rejection with a broken heart and spirit.

Biblical Example: Timothy

Timothy's faithful desire to serve the Church remains evident through his care and service to Paul and others. Paul wrote this about Timothy.

"I trust in the Lord Jesus to send Timothy shortly unto you... I have no man likeminded, who will naturally care for your state. For all seek their own, not the things which are Jesus Christ's. But ye know the proof of him, that, as a son with the father, he hath served with me in the gospel" (Philippians 2:19–22).

Ministers of Service: In the Spirit Vs in The Flesh

When working out of the Spirit, those with the motivation gift of service remain hyper-alert to recognizing needs within the church and within the lives of others. They radiate hospitality, generosity, and joy. Furthermore, they are very flexible, available, and filled with endurance to stay however long it takes to complete the task. On the contrary, when working out of the flesh; they become insensitive, lonely, isolated, stingy, pouting, resistant to change, and unavailable. Beyond that, they even may walk out on the job frustrated in the middle of the task; when operating out of the flesh.[21]

Do You Know Someone with the Gift of Service?

I am certain, you can identify someone in your life who possesses this gift. Remember, they desperately need to hear gratitude from you for what they are doing. Let them help you set the table when they are your guest; because, not to allow them to help only makes them feel useless. On the other hand, if they are interposing and their eagerness is pushing you into a corner; explain, gently to them that you really need them to just sit beside you instead of flittering around you. Example, maybe I need the person to sit beside

---

[21] Stanley, "Gifted," Part 3 Service

me and pray with me; instead, of washing my dishes. So, gently, I tell the person gifted with service my true needs; instead, of what they perceive I need. Then, thank them profoundly for what they have done for me. Thus, I avoid their frustration, in addition to my own read need going unanswered.

What If Service Is Your Motivational Gift?

First, thank you for all you do for the body of the church; promoting the gospel story through action.

Paul's Admonition: in Romans 12:7 to those with the gift of service "Or ministry, let us wait on our ministering". Why would Paul suggest those with the gift of service wait about ministering their service? Because, those with the gift of service tend to run in before asking God if that is the best thing to do. They see the need and don't stop to consider; that perhaps, God is using that need to teach the other person something about Himself. Therefore, the person with the gift of service; needs to pause long enough to pray and wait for God to give them the green light before jumping into service.

MERCY

God chose some to carry the torch of Mercy as their special spiritual gift. Those who bear this motivational gift see and feel the pain and sorrow of others. As they enter any gathering, they immediately see and make their way toward the sad, down trodden soul sitting off in the corner. Feeling their pain, the person gifted with Mercy is drawn like a magnet to their side. Likewise, the sad heart seeks out Mercy. I speak more personally of this gift; because, I have learned of its power and its deepest sorrow by living a lifetime with it. Until that fateful day that I heard Dr. Charles Stanley preach on the gift of Mercy from his series *"God's Children Gifted for Ministry"*; I had been a victim of my own spiritual gift.

A victim whose pathway lay strewn with shattered pieces of her own heart; because, I did not understand why I was drawn toward all the broken and down trodden hearts. Oh, yes; I knew and eluded joy throughout this journey; because, I knew my source of joy was God alone. Yet, at the same time I bore the scars of pain. For you see, those with the gift of Mercy are all in; therefore, they often feel rejected or unloved; because, few can respond with the same depth of love give. Those bearing this gift tend to see the good, the best that another person can be, if only they could see who God made them to be. Therefore, Mercy forgives whatever offence today; because, they know, if only the other person knew God's love; they wouldn't have caused such pain.

The Gift of Mercy, Where Joy and Sorrow Meet

Those with the motivational gift of Mercy live in a world where Sorrow and Joy meet

They spend hours on their knees alone with God; crying buckets of tears, to be restored. It would seem the oddity of all oddities; that, those whom God has gifted with the greatest capacity to love unconditionally would find themselves often the most solitary of all his children. Yet, in their solitude; God is their source of love, joy and hope. It took me nearly a lifetime to learn this truth; yet, knowledge is the key to carrying out your own special spiritual gift. Beyond that, I learned to understand the trials I faced. To learn true empathy, those with the gift of Mercy often face a lifetime of trials; preparing them to understand the pain of others.

Could I speak to another with chronic illness, if I never faced illness? Or cancer! Can I really understand or listen as well; if I had not walked a mile in their shoes? I learned: it wasn't God's anger that allowed so much tragedy in my life; instead, it was His love drawing me closer to Him and preparing me for the ministry He ordained me to walk in.

For you see, Mercy is the body of joy, love and forgiveness in the church. Often, they are misunderstood and criticized for not being strict enough at teaching discipline. Although, they understand and truly experience the harsh effects of evil in the world; at the same time, those with the gift of Mercy believe that no sinner is too far removed, but that God could save them.

Biblical Example: John

In all of John's writing (from the gospel of John to the three epistles of John); a unique perspective of Christ's ministry is presented. Always, John writes about the heart of the gospel being that of Grace and Love. He wrote:

> *A new commandment I give unto you, that ye love one another; as I have loved you, that ye also love one another. By this shall all men know that ye are my disciples, if ye have love one to another* (John 13:34-35).

Mercy: In the Spirit vs in the Flesh

When those with the gift of Mercy are working in the Spirit; they are attentive, sensitive, compassionate, fair, gentle, protective, meek, and willing to suffer. When working in the flesh, they are unconcerned, callus, partial, indifferent, harsh, rude and filled with anger. [22]

Do You Know Someone with The Gift of Mercy?

If indeed you see someone with the gift of Mercy, give them a smile and perhaps a hug. At times, they really need a leader or prophet to balance out their emotions; however, the one who steps in to help Mercy, must do so with love, kindness and a gentleness of spirit. Otherwise, Mercy will withdraw into a shell or worse, strike out against their would-be helpers.

If Mercy is Your Gift, Then What?

Paul's Admonition: in Romans 12 to those with Mercy "he that sheweth mercy, (do so) with cheerfulness." Why would Paul need to remind those with the motivational gift of Mercy to do so with cheerfulness? Ah, that's easy; because, those given the gift of mercy must face the evil, pain, and sorrow of this world; yielding a sword of love. Often, they walk through the darkest valleys and storms in this world; preparing for the battle that lies ahead of them. If your gift is mercy, be careful, when reaching down so low to pull others up; don't get pulled into the pit with them.

Also, beware of your own emotions. Not everyone God places in your path to love remain forever. So, be willing to let go when the task is complete without feeling broken. Also, be very careful; sometimes, people will confuse your acts of kindness for romantic love. You may even fall into this trap of seeking romance where it shouldn't be.

---

[22] Stanley, "Gifted," Part 8 Mercy

Giving (The Money Managers)

Those gifted by Christ with the motivational gift of giving know how to manage money well. They are very concerned with wisely managing the money to make the greatest impact to the most. They proficiently manage money, time, energy and creativity. This is quite different than what society would think; because, society would be concerned with the amount of giving. Whereas, the true spiritual gift of giving never is concerned with the amount as much as how that can be utilized to its fullest for the kingdom of God. Also, those with the gift of giving are very astute to differentiating true ministerial need from unwarranted use of the money.

Often, those with the gift of Giving; give anonymously; because their pleasure comes from act of giving, not the accolades of others. Because they gain their greatest pleasure from giving; often, they live very frugally to give more. They are sometimes misunderstood by those who call them tight fisted; which is the furthest from the truth. They make wise investments of their resources. When giving they do so with discernment, carefully choosing those in whom their investment will reap the most benefit. Hoaxers beware, those with the gift of Giving can spot you from miles away.

Those with the motivational gift of giving are motivated by God to give. Indeed, they hate high pressure tactics by others asking for their money; because, they need to evaluate the potential outcome first. Therefore, they are very thoughtful and prayerful about each gift; never, acting spontaneously. Furthermore, because they trust God to supply all their needs. They are both generous and the ones who can encourage others to give.

Biblical Example: Matthew

Of all the new testament scripture, there is more discussion regarding the wise usage of money in the gospel of Matthew. Also, he presents clearly the admonitions of Jesus against the Pharisees and the money changers regarding money and time management.

> *And whosoever shall compel thee to go a mile, go with him twain. Give to him that asketh thee, and from him that would borrow of thee turn not thou away* (Matthew 5:41-42).

GIFT OF GIVING: In the Spirit Vs in The Flesh

When working in the Spirit, those with the gift of giving are thrifty, resourceful, contented, punctual, cautious, tolerant and gratefulness. On the contrary, when they are walking in the flesh; they are extravagant, wasteful, covetous, tardy, rash, prejudiced, and ungrateful. [23]

Do You Know Someone with The Gift Of Giving?

If so, be careful not to be envious of their ease dealing with money, investing and finding the best bargain every time. Give them time to research any cause; before, they commit themselves or their money to them. Don't be disparaged when they enthusiastically encourage you to give; reminding you that God will take care of you. And certainly, never expect them to be reaching out a helping hand to you; simply, because you squandered your money. If they do help; they will expect to hand you a tight budget to follow so as not to be in this position again. Never forget how important those gifted with money management skills are to the furtherance of the gospel.

---

[23] Stanley, "Gifted," Part 6 Giving

If Giving is Your Gift, Then What?

Be patient with those of us who don't. Many of us love to give; but, lack the wisdom in giving. Personally, I am one of those. I have given away more than I have ever kept; however, I lack the discernment and wisdom to evaluate the best places to give. Also, I react spontaneously without patience. Every day I must pray that God guide my finances; despite me. I am getting better. But, if you, who has the gift of giving, meet me along the way; please, gently teach me how to be wiser in the management of my money.

Paul's Admonition: to those with the gift of giving: "let him do it with simplicity". In some scripture, the Greek word used here is translated to liberally; therefore, many have translated this as generously. However, another translation for the Greek word *haplotes* is to perform the task with a sincere heart or "singleness" of motive. With all that I have learned about the gift of giving; I believe it is the second warning Paul gives. In your love of giving, never allow pride or selfish desires for praise to enter your heart. Always, maintain the sincerity of heart toward God; knowing your gift is to Him, for Him and by Him.

Exhortation

Jesus calls some to encourage others into spiritual growth and maturity by gifting them with the special motivational gift of exhortation. Motivated by a passionate desire for others to grow in Christ; they delight in watching God's work flourish within the lives of others. Because they can see past all the mess of today, focusing on God's finished product; they urge the young believer on. They clearly

Effie Darlene Barba

discern the problems of faith and theology standing in the way of success; laying out a step by step process one must follow to achieve their fullest potential in Christ Jesus. Each step outlined is clearly based on Biblical Principles; with strict detail to accurate theology.

Before establishing the step by step plan, those with the gift of exhortation invest many hours of study. When they are one on one with those whom they are helping, they observe and analyze the problem prayerfully before developing the best plan. When those who are gifted with exhortation write or speak publicly, they often have either themselves lived through the problems or knew someone who did. That way they bring experience to the table. I see portraits of exhortation in the books of Lysa Terkeurst, as well as in her speaking style.

Exhorters See Trials as Merely Stepping Stones

Because they need to fully analyze the situation, developing the best plan; others criticize them for being too nosy or "in your face." This is particularly true when the person they are helping doesn't demonstrate any improvement or will to improve. At other times, they are thought to be insensitive or uncaring; because, they see trials as stepping stones to Glory.

Usually, much like mercy; those with the gift of Exhortation have themselves walked many a mile with trials and tribulations of their own. For that reason, they know the steps they want to teach someone are tried and true. Having walked the road; they know God is faithful to complete the work He began in each child.

Biblical Example: Paul

Certainly, Paul, himself was no stranger to pain, trials, and tribulations. He knew in detail each step necessary to grow in Christ. His desire always was to return and to see the growth accomplished in each believer. He rejoiced when he heard of their growth in the faith; urging them on with joyful glee.

Wherefore I also, after I heard of your faith in the Lord Jesus, and love unto all the saints, Cease not to give thanks for you, making mention of you in my prayers; That the God of our Lord Jesus Christ, the Father of glory, may give unto you the spirit of wisdom and revelation in the knowledge of him: The eyes of your understanding being enlightened; that ye may know what is the hope of his calling, and what the riches of the glory of his inheritance in the saints, And what is the exceeding greatness of his power to us-ward who believe, according to the working of his mighty power, Which he wrought in Christ, when he raised him from the dead (Ephesians 1:15-20).

Gift of Exhortation: In the Spirit Vs in The Flesh

When abiding in the Spirit; those with the gift of exhortation shine brightly with wisdom, discernment, faith, discretion, love, and enthusiasm. When the flesh reigns supreme in their life, they stand judgmental, critical, presumptive, simple minded, selfish, apathetic underachievers.[24]

Do You Know Someone with The Gift of Exhortation?

Most likely you have met or known someone with this gift, and if not; probably you should. Don't react defensively when they ask so many questions. They truly want to discover why you are struggling; thereby, developing a plan for you to grow in Christ Jesus. Also, they love to hear about your advancements in the knowledge of Christ. They even love to hear you talk about God and all that He taught you during the storms; because, they are ecstatic to see your growth in the knowledge of God.

If Exhortation Is Your Gift, Then What?

Learn to explain why you are asking so many questions. Be quick to share your own struggles with open vulnerability; demonstrating your understanding. When you share your own failures or trials, it opens the door for others to be open and honest as well. Whatever, God has walked you through has purpose and value in helping others to grow from your journey.

Paul's Admonition:

Or he that exhorteth, on exhortation Rejoicing in hope; patient in tribulation; continuing instant in prayer Rejoice with them that do

---

[24] Stanley, "Gifted," Part 5 Exhortation

rejoice, and weep with them that weep.
(Romans 12:8,12,15).

Appeal to the heart of those you are striving to help, not just the mind; drawing a brother or sister in Christ aside, encouraging them each step of the way. Always, willing to walk beside them; however long it takes.

Teacher

Those with the Motivational Gift of Teaching are focused on truth, accuracy, and detail. They study each word in three categories. First, the definition of the word itself. Second, how it fits in the context with the scriptures surrounding it. Third, they want to know how it fits doctrinally with the rest of the Bible. Researching, studying for hours; they are most fulfilled by having discovered the truth. Meanwhile, they are quick to hear heresy and to speak out against it with solid, sound arguments based on scripture.

Designed by God to keep us doctrinally sound; they play a vital role in the body of Christ. Yet, because their greatest joy comes from discovering and proving the truth; they may not seem as interested in people as they are in knowledge. This can cause them to appear distant or calculating; while listening more than talking. Their brain constantly sorting and filing the information flowing in; they are very attentive to every detail.

Because they focus on detailed truth; often, they are falsely seen as too critical. Their passionate patience to discover every detail of truth before acting; others see as procrastination; although really it is not. Those with the gift of Teaching believe: "fools rush in where angels fear to trod."

Example in The Bible: Luke

Luke had a very specific eye for detail, researching the truth before writing. Clearly, we see this in both the Gospel of Luke as well as in the Acts of the Apostle.

> *Dear friend who loves God——Several biographies of Christ have already been written using as their source material the reports circulating among us from the early disciples and other eyewitnesses. However, it occurred to me that it would be well to recheck all these accounts from first to last and after thorough investigation to pass this summary on to you to reassure you of the truth of all you were taught.* (Luke 1:2 4, TLB)

With the investigative skills of a researcher, Luke checked and rechecked the information he obtained for accuracy before writing his gospel account Jesus' life. Certainly, God authored the writings of the Bible; but, in this case chose someone gifted as a Teacher to pen the words. Not everyone with the Motivational Gift of Teaching are teachers; many are lawyers and physicians. Remember Luke was a physician.

Gift of Teaching: In the Spirit vs In the Flesh

Disciplined, confident, reverent, diligent, thorough, and patient describes those with the gift of teaching, when walking in the Spirit. Whenever they are walking in the flesh, they display self-indulgence, slothfulness, anxiety, restlessness, fragmented, and unpredictable.[25]

Do You Know Someone with The Gift of Teaching?

Don't be surprised! They aren't always working as teachers. Many of the best teachers have other motivational gifts such as exhortation or mercy; however, when they are Professional Teachers, most likely they are Professors. Glean from their knowledge base and don't be offended when they challenge yours. Their questions and debates urge you to search and discover the truth for yourself. Be willing to question and prayerfully study yourself to determine if they are accurate or if they have somehow faltered in their interpretation.

If Teaching is Your Gift, Then What?

Sometimes your love of knowledge can lead you toward philosophies or teachings that really don't represent the truth of Gospel. Remain steadfast in prayer, always seeking God's wisdom to discern the truth, as you carefully dissect each word. Also, be aware that your knowledge is wonderful to have; but, teaching the truth to others builds the church. For that reason, don't keep your torch hidden under a basket.

Paul's Admonition: Those with the gift "of teaching, teach." It is good to research, study and discover the truth. Even though that has satisfied your desires, providing great pleasure; don't forget to share that knowledge by teaching others along the way.

---

[25] Stanley, "Gifted," Part 4 Teaching

Prophecy (Justice)

Enter the brave, the bold defenders of truth and justice! Those with the gift of Prophecy stand tall; boldly defending truth and speaking out against injustice. They fight against evil, hypocrisy, and bigotry. Quick to recognize injustice, they speak out for truth. Because, in their eyes, the world has no shades of compromise allowed, either things are right or wrong. Rejecting evil, they are quick to point out their own failures and frailties. Disciplined and determined, they put on the whole armor of God to battle against evil forces.

Those with the gift of prophecy can be very persuasive, very direct when confronting what they see as sin in another's life, and want to see immediate change or repentance. They view trials and even brokenness as blessing in disguise; because they recognize that often it is brokenness which drives us to our knees and closer to Christ. For that reason, they see trials as hidden opportunities for spiritual growth. Therefore, they do not moan, whine or complain when trials come into their life; because, they can see the blessings they still possess. Knowing clearly their own faults; they see every blessing in their life as an act of Grace from God. After all, they remember: were it not for grace, they deserved wrath and condemnation.

The Brave, The Bold Defenders of Truth and Justice

So easily misjudged as harsh, outspoken, and intolerant; those with the gift of Prophecy (Justice) appear impulsive. Yet, they truly are harsher on themselves than on anyone else. Loyal to the end, they stand up against the bullies to defend the weaker sheep.

Their greatest desire: to save you from the consequences of sin in your life; by helping you see the folly, repent and transform your heart and mind through the power of God's Grace toward you. For them, they see this as a simple: acknowledge your sin and stop the perpetuation of it NOW!

Biblical Example: Peter

Impetuous, out spoken, passionate Peter; one building block leading the way for the early church. Always aware of his own failures; Peter stood firm on truth and justice within the body of Christ. While at the same time, Peter gave all the credit to God; where it belonged.

> *Knowing this first, that no prophecy of the scripture is of any private interpretation. For the prophecy came not in old time by the will of man: but holy men of God spake as they were moved by the Holy Ghost* (I Peter 1:20-21).

Gift of Prophecy: In the Spirit vs in the Flesh

When living in the Spirit, they display unyielding commitment to truth, obedience, sincerity, virtue, and boldness in the authority of the word of God. Furthermore, they are quick to forgive someone who wants to change, in addition, to being persuasive and loyal. When they get out of the spirit, allowing the flesh to rule; beware! They are deceptive, rebellious, hypocritical, defiled, fearful, resentful of others and manipulative.[26]

---

[26] Stanley, "Gifted," Part 2 Prophecy

Do You Know Someone with The Gift of Prophecy?

I am certain you have met someone quick to strike out against any injustice they see! Ah, as your eyes roll and you take that deep sign; I know you have. Yet, let me suggest; you open your eyes to realize their wondrous value, their passion and their heart. That outward exterior of harshness covers a heart that desires your best. They want to protect you from the harms of this world and from yourself at times. We all need one prophet in our lives, who can step in to defend us against injustice and to turn us around when we start down some road of compromise.

If Prophecy is Your Gift, Then What?

Pray for patience and practice verbal self-control. Remain sensitive to the responses of others around you. Remember to act out of the spirit in love, working to the edification of the other; but, never be ashamed of the gift you were given. Every church needs at least one Prophet to hold everyone else accountable. I daresay, every family needs at least one to defend, protect and admonish when we need to be admonished.

Paul's Admonition: "*But he that prophesieth speaketh unto men to edification, and exhortation, and comfort*" (I Corinthians 14:3). Remember your role in the body of Christ to guide others toward moral excellence, encourage them along their journey, and comfort them when they fall. Help them to rise again to face a brand-new day.

CONCLUSIONS:

I realize that I have belabored our way through the various Motivational Gifts of the Spirit. Furthermore, our gifts come as part of the bigger identity: our position in Christ Jesus. We have gone through the positions that are ours in Christ Jesus as God's Beloved, Blessed, Chosen, Redeemed Child, heir of the kingdom, Servant by choice, Enlightened, New Creation, Declared Saint, Mighty Warrior and Gifted follower. In each position granted us in Christ Jesus, we are immediately made whole; except in that of our Motivational Gift. Why would that be? Because God is wise; He knew our heart's tendency to pride, so He made certain no one could stand alone as an island.

One Body, Many Parts

Companionship, interdependence, and communion are necessary components for the gospel to be spread and the church to thrive and grow. Therefore, God gave gifts to men in a manner to ascertain the growth of the church, as they work together.

> *But unto every one of us is given grace according to the measure of the gift of Christ. Wherefore he saith, "When he ascended up on high, he led captivity captive, and gave gifts unto men" (Ephesians 4:7-8).*

Everyone Has a Spiritual Motivational Gift

Everyone who accepted Christ as their Savior has a spiritual motivational gift; whether we know it or not. Jesus purchased this on Calvary and; then, brought it to fruition with His resurrection. No one has been excluded. For that reason, we do need to study, learn of our own gift. I urge you to get Charles Stanley's series, "God's Children Gifted for Ministry".

In the following Chapter, I do want to point out the importance of learning to love and honor each other's gifts through understanding the intricate functions of the many parts of God's Church.

Because this chapter may have gotten a tidbit tedious, I have written you this poem to remind you of each motivational gift of the Spirit.

Abiding Steadfast Joy

Gifts of the Spirit

The Prophet with His Sword doth stand
Reminding us of God's command
To live a life of Righteousness
That we might find in God our Bliss

The teacher doth research each word
Discovering when men speak absurd
To never, ever compromise
That through God's Word we can be wise

As Mercy comes with Gift of Grace
A smile of joy across her face
Searching for broken hearts she finds
Each cut and scar with love she binds

While service works from morn to night
Wanting each part to be just right
Seeking evermore to please
A thank you puts their heart at ease

Exhorter comes with comfort praise

To help each one their spirit raise

With steps designed as one, two, three

To follow close, your heart to free

The Giver comes with cautious eye

Needing to know the how and why

A Brilliant Mind, a financier

Who saves, to give then without fear

And then there is the one who leads

Who cannot hear naysayers pleads

The focus always straight ahead

Complete the task as God has led.

Effie Darlene Barba

Chapter 30:

United We Stand

It was February 4, 2010. My mind was in a spiraling whirlwind of emotions, alone. Helplessness, sorrow, anger, guilt, fatigue, fear and even love were all jumbled in my brain as I wrote a blog post that day called, "What do I do when I am lost in a sea of craziness?" Mom was in the hospital with a psychotic breakdown. It wasn't the first; but, it did seem the worst she had experienced over the course of the time I had been taking care of her. Beyond that, exhausted and broke, I feared a financial collapse. Having spent way beyond my means to provide private sitters for mom to avoid this breakdown; it came anyway. I was drowning emotionally, physically, and financially. Unless someone reached out a helping hand to rescue me, I might not survive.

As all the mixed emotions were whirling in my head, I began to wonder "where is the fine line between sanity and insanity?" I "carried the torch for Christ, for my family, and for work, alone" I thought.

That day, I wondered; "Really, am I so different from Mom? Don't I have fears, sorrows, worries, and moments of depression? "The only difference between mom and me." I thought. "I hold my emotions tightly hidden deep within; whereas, she wears her emotions like a banner of honor; as though her diagnosis gave her the freedom to do or say whatever she pleased." I, on the other hand; got up, went to work, strove to say the right things, struggled to pay all the bills for both of us, cleaned the house, stood responsibly; while clinging tight to the final shred of hope. And then try to forgive myself when I failed to get it all done. Angry, tired and desperate; I was drowning in my own thoughts and emotions. That wasn't even the worst of where I stood that day, feeling so alone, despairing and truly frightened.

WHEN LOST AND ALONE

Furthermore, I hated myself for allowing such a thought to enter my brain. After all, there was mom completely lost into a psychotic world and I so unsympathetic; thinking of only my own pain. Yet, the pain ran so deep; I only wanted to run. Praying fervently: I pleaded with God, even though I had no idea what to pray. If God is with me; then, He is all I need, right? Then why did I feel so all alone.

GOD SENT A HELPING HAND

I learned a valuable lesson the next day when I received a call from Alberto, my son. He had read the blog and suddenly knew that he must intervene with a word of truth. He called to give me a reality check.

"Mom, listen to me." He was very firm and strong as he began to outline the truth of my identity in Christ Jesus. He reminded me of the ministry I had been called to do and that I must stand on the truth of "who I am in Christ Jesus". "Quit listening to Satan's lies. Pull it together", he commanded.

Then with a gentler voice, he said; "Mom, I love you, you are stronger than this and you know the truth of God's strength in you. You have been through a lot worse with God's guidance. So, why would you, now, let your testimony be destroyed over something you have no control over? I don't understand; because, I wish I had the testimony of strength you do. You have the power of God in you to control your response to the situation at hand; so, use it. By the way, I am not the one who is the best listener. So, if you need someone to listen, call Ron or Melissa. Love you." With that, he hung up.

NOT ALONE

Suddenly, I realized that I was not a force of one. As I reflected on what had happened, I realized that God designed our pilgrimage journey on this earth in such a manner as to need each other.

EPHESIANS 4:4-7,16 (TLB)

We are all parts of one body, we have the same Spirit, and we have all been called to the same glorious future. For us there is only one Lord, one faith, one baptism, and we all have the same God and Father who is over us all and in us all, and living through every part of us. However, Christ has given each of us special abilities ... Under his direction, the whole body is fitted together perfectly, and each part in its own special way helps the other parts, so that the whole body is healthy and growing and full of love.

NEEDING EACH OTHER

When Christ, ascended He gave gifts to men. Yet, God so designed the gifts in a manner that we all need each other. He did not give you or me all the gifts; allowing us to stand alone. Each of us hold one primary motivational gift. For the work of the church to grow and prosper, we need all the spiritual gifts working in harmony. That means, we need each other.

Jesus Christ, chose your unique spiritual gift; just as He did mine and every individual one who makes up His body, the church.

> But unto every one of us is given grace according to the measure of the gift of Christ. Wherefore he saith, 'When he ascended up on high, he led captivity captive, and gave gifts unto men' (Ephesians 4:7-8).

Harmoniously, united we stand strong. No one stands alone. Together, in love we become a force that cannot be destroyed when storms surround us. Each reaching out in love, we strengthen each other.

That day, Alberto stepped out of his comfort zone and God for a moment equipped him with the gift of exhortation; although, his primary gifts are leadership and giving (equally). Yes, sometimes God allows us to utilize other gifts in moments of crisis; as, He did that day. And, yes; some people have two gifts equally balanced; when, God so chooses.

When we try to stand alone, we often become angry, embittered and lose perspective. God designed His church, so we would need each other. He did the same within the family. We need to learn how to value each other's uniqueness in the body of the church, the family and the community; reaching out our hands in love and unity

KNOWLEDGE IS KEY TO HARMONY

All too often, we misunderstand each other because we want to see everyone through our own narrowed lens of perception. As Christ ascended on high, he gave gifts to men. Although, Jesus Christ is the perfect embodiment of all the Spiritual Motivational Gifts, when He gave these to us within the church, the gifts were divided. Since each of us may see the world through differing lenses, we need to learn how to see the whole body of the church clearly. This can only happen through understanding each other's motivational gifts. Once we see the power and beauty of each gift, we can embrace the differences with open arms; realizing we need each other's gift.

This is true both in the Church and in the family. When we combine the various gifts harmoniously, we develop a strong defensive line against attack by outside forces of any kind, including from satanic attack. For us to work harmoniously, we must first understand and appreciate, "where we are coming from". That is why we find so much bickering and dispute within our families and our churches. When I first heard Charles Stanley's series *God's Children Gifted for Ministry*, it changed my dynamics within the family, among my friends, at church, at work and even how I see others I meet along this journey.

ONE BODY MANY PARTS

As a unit, no member of the body is more important than another. It requires all the various members of the body harmoniously performing their unique part in an action. For a runner to train, he cannot say I will train my muscles; yet, forget the importance of his heart, lungs, eyes, ears, nose, skeletal system, brain and even arms. Each performs its own unique function, so the runner can perform at his or her best performance.

Paul wrote extensively about the variance in gifts and the importance of harmoniously working together in

1 CORINTHIANS 12:4-7 (TLB)

Now God gives us many kinds of special abilities, but it is the same Holy Spirit who is the source of them all. There are different kinds of service to God, but it is the same Lord we are serving. There are many ways in which God works in our lives, but it is the same God who does the work in and through all of us who are his. The Holy Spirit displays God's power through each of us as a means of helping the entire church.

12-22 (TLB)

Our bodies have many parts, but the many parts make up only one body when they are all put together. So it is with the "body" of Christ. Each of us is a part of the one body of Christ. Some of us are Jews, some are Gentiles, some are slaves, and some are free. But the Holy Spirit has fitted us all together into one body. We have been baptized into

Christ's body by the one Spirit, and have all been given that same Holy Spirit.

Yes, the body has many parts, not just one part. If the foot says, "I am not a part of the body because I am not a hand," that does not make it any less a part of the body. And what would you think if you heard an ear say, "I am not part of the body because I am only an ear and not an eye"? Would that make it any less a part of the body? Suppose the whole body were an eye—then how would you hear? Or if your whole body were just one big ear, how could you smell anything?

But that isn't the way God has made us. He has made many parts for our bodies and has put each part just where he wants it. What a strange thing a body would be if it had only one part! So he has made many parts, but still there is only one body.

The eye can never say to the hand, "I don't need you." The head can't say to the feet, "I don't need you."

And some of the parts that seem weakest and least important are really the most necessary.

27 (TLB)

Now here is what I am trying to say: All of you together are the one body of Christ, and each one of you is a separate and necessary part of it.

ONE FAMILY STRONG WITH DIFFERENCES

So, let me try to demonstrate by example; how, this functions by exposing my own family and our dynamics. There was a time; before, I listened to Charles Stanley's tapes that I found our interworking dynamics at times difficult to say the least; because of our wide differences. Certainly, we could cause each other as much harm as good; so, we pent up a lot of emotions; because, we just didn't know how the other one thinks so differently and responds so differently. Now, I know what a blessing and gift from God our differences truly are.

Earlier I related a story about a moment in time when I was drowning emotionally, financially, and ultimately spiritually; because, I tried to do it all without talking to my children at all. My reasoning: to avoid burdening them with my problems. Yet, I was drowning; with nowhere to turn; never realizing that God had already equipped my family with everything we ever needed to stand strong against Satan.

MERCY

My gift: Mercy. Mercy needs a protector and a wise counselor to survive! I knew the struggles deep within my own heart; yet, could never fully comprehend them until I heard Charles Stanley's sermon that day on Mercy. Yes, Mercy is the bright, shining light of hope, joy, and unwavering faith; however, Mercy is always getting tangled up in the "how to" and "when's" of helping others in this life. Always giving money, I did not have, to help others who did not or could not change; I needed help. I begged God for discernment, which never came. Little did I know; my own son was the one who could rescue me from myself; if I only learned to confess and listen. He could devise the plan for success.

GIVING

Alberto has that gift of discernment regarding money. He can find the best bargain, know when to spend and when not to. Brilliantly, he manages his money so that he is positioned to give to God's work; yet, even that he does with careful discernment that his money will have the greatest impact on the world. Recognizing his gift, I should have been open to listening; yet, I daresay, my own fear of losing his respect, drove away. after all, if he knew how foolish his mom was; would he still love me? Of course, the truth is: he always knew and respectfully didn't say anything. That is until, I was moving to Missouri and he said, "Mom, my guess you don't have the down payment for a house and yours in Florida is underwater. So, I will buy you a house; you make the monthly payments. Love you." And that was that.

LEADERSHIP:

Alberto also has a second motivational gift: leadership. In the case of our family, some would need to carry two for our survival. He sees the big picture and can focus on completing the task. For that same reason, he does not accept the emotions which interfere with moving forward.

His philosophy: "Never listen to the naysayers; because, negativity stops the progress." Also, he truly is the "forgetting that which is behind" (Philippians 3:13), press forward kind of guy. Every family needs at least one. He always says, "Mom, I love you. I am here; but, if you need someone to listen, Call Ron or Melissa." He knows his limitations; yet, if we need someone to complete any project or to pull us forward, it is Alberto we turn to.

JUSTICE:

Ron's Gift is Justice. He quickly can see any situation with clarity, knowing right and wrong. Also, he is very persuasive at laying out the argument as to why or why not to proceed. Along with that means, he listens astutely to all that is said, filing and dissecting it with accuracy. Then, when he pronounces his judgement of the situation; he presents it clearly, like a prosecutor laying out his case. At the same time, he has a slight touch of Mercy sprinkled in; making him the "go to guy" for any tough decisions. However, as the case for those with the gift of justice; he can be way too harsh on himself as well.

SERVICE:

Melissa's gift is clearly service. Always available, she flitters about serving and helping. Quick to always be ready to help anywhere, everywhere and anybody who needs her to. She would drop everything to run to my side if I needed her there. The best friend on the phone, always ready to listen and serve with kindness. Before, I failed to recognize her needs for gratitude and demonstrations of love in return; yet, I am learning each day how to give back what she needs. Well at least, sometimes. Still working on that; because, those with the gift of service need to know they are appreciated fully.

TEACHING:

Perhaps, lurking in the background; I had a touch of this gift, always studying in search of truth both in God's Word and life. Although, I must say; a busy life allowed complacency. Yet, I have found the motivational gift of teaching is increasing in its significance in my life. Now the busier I am, the more time I also devote to Bible Study. Now, I yearn to spend hours "rightly dividing the truth" (2 Timothy 2:15). The point there being that as we grow in Christ, we may gain another Motivational Gift of the Spirit taking on a much higher role than it did in the past. Studying God's word and sharing that through my writing and speaking have become one of my greatest pleasures in life, now as I get older. Well, and with age; I have grown a bit more patient, allowing me to fill my hours with studying God's word and growing in the knowledge of Him.

EXHORTATION:

I cannot say that any of us in my little family have this one; however, each of us have been granted it when needed in a moment of crisis. Remember Jesus Christ holds all the Motivational Gifts; therefore, can fill us as needed for a situation we are facing. Much like when Alberto called me to say "Mom, this is what you need to do!"; while laying out a perfect 3 step plan as how to do it.

CONCLUDING THOUGHTS:

So, there you have it. Just as God graciously equipped my family with all the gifts; He does His Church. Also, knowledge of how these each work is key to harmony in the family and in the church. I hope I have at least whet your appetite to learn more about the Spiritual Motivational gifts and encourage you to get Charles Stanley sermon series. It

Effie Darlene Barba

can change the dynamics of your home, church, work and where ever you go for the good. United we stand, always with greater strength, hope, and joy.

Chapter 31:

THEREFORE…In Christ I am His

Throughout this section of the book, we have looked deeply into the position we hold in Christ Jesus; our true identity. Guaranteed by God Himself, the covenant written and signed by the blood of Christ Jesus and sworn to by God upon His Word (Hebrews 6:13-20). Yet, if we do not write them on our hearts, we forget. As the hustle and bustle of this world tugs at our hearts, it would seem amnesia occurs; because, we forget or never even count as ours the innumerable possessions we hold in Christ Jesus.

In Christ, I am God's chosen, beloved, redeemed, blessed child-heir of His Kingdom. Beyond that I am His declared saint, gracious servant of Perfect love; born into perfect righteousness as God's new creation in Christ Jesus. Furthermore, I am equipped as a Mighty Warrior and enlightened with His wisdom by the work of the Holy Spirit living within me. And if that were not enough, I am also gifted with a special spiritual motivational gift to drive my missionary endeavors as I join hands United with those God places in my path bearing other gifts. Thus, He has provided me with community as well.

IS KNOWLEDGE ENOUGH?

Knowing all this, should mean I stand strong and firm in every situation of life! However, just knowing this in my head; doesn't mean I believe it in my heart. That head/heart disconnect is what leads to fears, doubt, anxiety and even depression within the life of the Christian. Our life depends upon our knowing unequivocally our position in Christ Jesus; bought and sealed by the blood of Christ Himself.

So, how do I transform that head knowledge into undeniable truth written upon my heart? Well, let me propose there are 7 steps to this process

1. Accept Jesus Christ as Your Lord and Savior
2. Prayerfully Study God's Word
3. Declare it as So
4. Realize Every Trial is a lesson in Truth
5. Keep a Faith Journal
6. Seek Godly Counselors When Doubt Arises
7. Rest Assured, God Will Write it on Your Heart

ACCEPT JESUS CHRIST AS YOUR LORD AND SAVIOR

If you do not know Jesus Christ as your Savior, that is the first step. Everything, including your eternity; hinges on that truth.

> *For God so loved the world, that he gave his only begotten Son, that whosoever believeth in him should not perish, but have everlasting life* (John 3:16)

> *If any man thirst, let him come unto me, and drink. He that believeth on me, as the scripture hath said, out of his belly shall flow rivers of living water* (John 7:37-38).

Where ever you are, come right now! Bow your head and ask Jesus to come into your heart, confessing that you are a sinner in need of His Saving Grace; believing that He is God's Son who died and rose again to pay the price for your sin. Then just say, "Thank You, Lord Jesus"

PRAYERFULLY STUDY GOD'S WORD

God provided us with the truth of Himself in His Word. They are His Love letters to us.

For the word of God is alive and powerful. It is sharper than the sharpest two-edged sword, cutting between soul and spirit, between joint and marrow. It exposes our innermost thoughts and desires (Hebrews 4:12 NLT).

Study to shew thyself approved unto God, a workman that needeth not to be ashamed, rightly dividing the word of truth (2 Timothy 2:14-16).

With my whole heart have I sought thee: O let me not wander from thy commandments. Thy word have I hid in mine heart, that I might not sin against thee (Psalm 119:10-11).

If you really want to know God, then study His Word. It is alive and powerful to transform your heart to trust Him more.

DECLARE IT AS SO

Stand before your mirror and declare this truth. Shout it before the crowd; humbly, acknowledging your position in Christ Jesus, by grace alone. Yet, do not confuse this for pridefully declaring "I AM" as some modernistic preachers have done. Instead, like Louie Giglio, say; "*I am not but I know I AM*".[27] Therefore, I am God's Blessed, Beloved, Chosen, Redeemed Child; because of all Jesus Christ did for me on the Cross and not my works of my own hands.

I will declare the decree: the LORD hath said unto me, 'Thou art my Son; this day have I begotten thee' (Psalm 2:7).

I will declare thy name unto my brethren: in the midst of the congregation will I praise thee (Psalm 22:22).

The more you hear yourself declaring the truth; (whether to yourself or to others in testimony) the more you will believe the truth in your own heart.

REALIZE EVERY TRIAL IS A LESSON IN TRUTH

God is Sovereign! Therefore, because He is Sovereign; every trial that enters your life came sifted through His Hands of Love. He allows trials, sorrows and pain in the

---

[27]Louie Giglio, *i am not but i know I AM,* (Sister's, OR: Multinomah Publishers, 2005)

life of His children that He might grow them up and they might come to know Him in the fullness of His Glory.

> *My brethren, count it all joy when ye fall into divers temptations; Knowing this, that the trying of your faith worketh patience. But let patience have her perfect work, that ye may be perfect and entire, wanting nothing* (James 1: 2-4).

> *So be truly glad! There is wonderful joy ahead, even though the going is rough for a while down here. These trials are only to test your faith, to see whether or not it is strong and pure. It is being tested as fire tests gold and purifies it—and your faith is far more precious to God than mere gold* (I Peter 1:6-7 TLB).

God allows our trials for our ultimate joy to be full. I know this; because, I have lived it and have seen it so in so many precious saints of the kingdom.

> *For which cause we faint not; but though our outward man perish, yet the inward man is renewed day by day. For our light affliction, which is but for a moment, worketh for us a far more exceeding and eternal weight of glory; While we look not at the things which are seen, but at the things which are not seen: for the things which are seen are temporal; but*

the things which are not seen are eternal (2 Corinthians 4:16-18).

His plan is for our good. His love allows no less than our fullness of joy; but, that sometimes mean we let go of counterfeit joys to find He is our Treasure and our Joy. His promise to each of us is.

> *we know that all things work together for good to them that love God, to them who are the called according to his purpose. For whom he did foreknow, he also did predestinate to be conformed to the image of his Son, that he might be the firstborn among many brethren. Moreover whom he did predestinate, them he also called: and whom he called, them he also justified: and whom he justified, them he also glorified. What shall we then say to these things? If God be for us, who can be against us?* Romans 8:28-31

KEEP A FAITH JOURNAL

I cannot stress enough the importance of doing this. Keep a journal of trials you face, the scriptures relating to the trial and God's ultimate deliverance from the trial. You will find that God did much more than deliver you, He carried you through and brought you precious gifts of faith, joy and hope you never dreamed of having.

Throughout the Old Testament, God urges His people to remember how He parted the Red sea, brought them out of captivity, provided them with manna, and how He delivered them repeatedly. He instructed them to write songs, pass them down from generation to generation lest they forget His love, His kindness and His faithfulness.

Let not mercy and truth forsake thee: bind them about thy neck; write them upon the table of thine heart: So shalt thou find favour and good understanding in the sight of God and man (Proverbs 3:3-4).

We, must do the same and pass it on to the generations beyond us. How could I not pass on God's faithfulness to my children, grandchildren and all the generations to follow? Journaling is one way of doing just that. Another is to write little notes in your favorite Bible, reminding you and any who will later read it of God's faithfulness to you.

SEEK GODLY COUNSELORS WHEN DOUBT ARISES

There are moments when we need help. Remember, our motivational gifts vary and there are times we need the help and guidance of another's gifts. Or, at other times; we just need a listening ear with an empathetic heart. I cannot tell you how often, God has sent just the right person into my life or the right sermon the moment I needed it. Sometimes in the most unlikely places, He has sent His message to me. One timely word spoken the moment I needed to hear it.

God sent counsellors to His people. Sometimes, prophets or priests; yet, we know at other times; God sent men. We know very little about David's uncle; except, this:

> *Jonathan David's uncle was a counsellor, a wise man* (I Chronicle 27:32)

We need counsellors at times. At other times, we need guidance from those gifted with special motivational gifts. However, we need to be careful to choose counselors who know God and are diligent to proclaiming truth.

REST ASSURED, GOD WILL WRITE IT ON YOUR HEART

And last; but, certainly not least. God has promised to write His precepts on your heart.

> *Whereof the Holy Ghost also is a witness to us: for after that he had said before, This is the covenant that I will make with them after those days, saith the Lord, I will put my laws into their hearts, and in their minds will I write them; And their sins and iniquities will I remember no more* (Hebrews 10:15-17).

> *Jesus saith unto her, Said I not unto thee, that, if thou wouldest believe, thou shouldest see the glory of God?* (John 11:40).

> *God of our Lord Jesus Christ, the Father of glory, may give unto you the spirit of wisdom*

and revelation in the knowledge of him: The eyes of your understanding being enlightened; that ye may know what is the hope of his calling, and what the riches of the glory of his inheritance in the saints, And what is the exceeding greatness of his power to us-ward who believe (Ephesians 1:17-19)

It may be through fiery trials, He reveals Himself. Or it may be through tiny glimpses of His Glory. We need to remain always open to seeing Him in every detail of our lives. Either way, He will complete the work He began in us; one day.

CONCLUDING THOUGHTS

I have tried to lay out for you some practical steps toward knowing the position you hold in Christ Jesus. My prayer remains, God open Your eyes to see Him; thereby, filling your life with overflowing fountains of joy, hope and love whatever may be your circumstances today.

Effie Darlene Barba

BECAUSE OF ALL THIS: JOY

Effie Darlene Barba

Chapter 32:

KNOWING THESE FOUNDATIONAL TRUTHS; NOW WHAT?

Throughout this book, I have laid out the case step by step concerning these three foundations on which to build your faith and your life upon. Beyond just knowing these truths in your mind; they must be indelibly written upon your heart. Because God knows it is imperative that we learn these truths; our life's journey often takes us through dark and treacherous valleys. It is in the depth of those valleys, God teaches us the truth of His Glory, His Sovereignty and His love toward us. Patiently preparing and equipping us with His truth, God guides us each step of the way; because, He knows that we can only find true joy, peace, and hope in a close and intimate relationship with Him.

Whatever trials, sorrows or temptations you face in this life; I can assure you of this: knowing these three foundations of truth will hold your heart steady, filling you with everlasting hope, steadfast joy, peace, and strength to live victoriously. Knowing these three truths; building upon them as your foundation gives you the power to remain fearless, steadfast, and joy filled no matter what storms come your way in this life: Never again to be bound in a life of quiet desperation.

First, know your place in this world; because, faith is knowing God IS (Supreme Creator, Sovereign Lord, the Being without which nothing else exists) and He rewards those who diligent seek Him. Second, you must realize your purpose in this world. God created you desiring to shower upon you His love, to fill you with His Joy, and to bestow upon you part of His Glory (though undeserving you may be). Thirdly, you must know your position in Christ Jesus;

held firm by the power of His resurrection; endowing you with the power to live victoriously.

WISDOM WRITTEN ON YOUR HEART

> *My son, forget not my law; but let thine heart keep my commandments: For length of days, and long life, and peace, shall they add to thee. Let not mercy and truth forsake thee: bind them about thy neck; write them upon the table of thine heart: So shalt thou find favour and good understanding in the sight of God and man. Trust in the Lord with all thine heart; and lean not unto thine own understanding. In all thy ways acknowledge him, and he shall direct thy paths* (Proverbs 3:1-6)

> *The Lord by wisdom hath founded the earth; by understanding hath he established the heavens. By his knowledge the depths are broken up, and the clouds drop down the dew. My son, let not them depart from thine eyes: keep sound wisdom and discretion: So, shall they be life unto thy soul, and grace to thy neck. Then shalt thou walk in thy way safely, and thy foot shall not stumble* (Proverbs 3:19-23)

SOLID ROCK FOUNDATIONS of LIFE

Truth must make its way from my mind into the depth of my heart; before, it becomes a foundation strong, steady, and unshifting. For a simple path of loose dirt or sand to become formed into solid rock, it undergoes great stress and then pressure. The waves crash against the shore, washing;

changing and transforming sand and debris into what is called a sedimentary rock. Because of extreme pressure, rock is formed. Igneous rocks form by undergoing extreme heating, melting and then, cooling. Because of the extreme stress they endure, they become firm, unmovable. Diamond formation occurs in extreme temperatures, extreme pressure over millions of years. Often, it is through our trials, sorrows, temptations and pains; we discover the solid foundations of knowing the truth of our place in the universe, our purpose, and our position in Christ Jesus

Living a life filled with peace, joy, hope, and fearless faith; comes from having lived through the harsh trials and learning to lean into an Almighty God. He is the truth, the way and the life. He is joy overflowing. I know this truth; because, through many trials; God wrote these truths indelibly into my heart. My journey has not been easy; however, I would walk every step of it again, knowing God's plan for me has always been for my good, His pleasure and my pleasure to be found in Him.

quote from Jonathan Edwards.

"Men have a great deal of pleasure in human knowledge, in studies of natural things; but this is nothing to that joy which arises from divine light shining into the soul. This spiritual light is the dawning of the light of glory in the heart. There is nothing so powerful as this to support persons in affliction, and to give the mind peace and brightness in this stormy and dark world. This knowledge will wean from the world, and raise the inclination to heavenly things. It will turn the heart to God as the fountain of good, and to choose him for the only portion. This light, and this only, will

> *bring the soul to a saving close with Christ. It conforms the heart to the gospel, mortifies its enmity and opposition against the scheme of salvation therein revealed: it causes the heart to embrace the joyful tidings, and entirely to adhere to, and acquiesce in the revelation of Christ as our Savior."[28]*

And so, dear pilgrim; do not despair. Do you know Jesus Christ as your Savior and Lord? It all begins there! For if you do not know the sweetness of His presence, His grace; then, there is reason for despair. I cannot imagine my life without Him. Yet, if you know Him; He will guide you and lead you to green meadows beside the still waters. Perhaps, for me; that journey has been through many mountainous terrains and raging oceanic storms; yet, it brought me to this place of abiding, steadfast joy. Glimpses of God's Glory have shone before me; leading me every step of the way. As I look back, I thank God for His wondrous Grace, Love and Mercy toward me which has brought me to this place of Abiding, Steadfast Joy: never again to be bound in a life of desperation.

---

[28] Jonathan Edwards, *A Divine and Supernatural Light, immediately imparted to the Soul by the Spirit of God, shown to be both a Scriptural, and Rational Doctrine-in a Sermon, 1734*, Digital Commons @ University of Nebraska-Lincoln, accessed October 28, 2017,
http://digitalcommons.unl.edu/cgi/viewcontent.cgi?article=10 56&context=etas

A TALK WITH GOD

Oh, let me Lord Delight in You
And lay all else I hold aside
For no desire could mean as much
As hear Your voice, to feel your touch
And in Your arms abide

I feel the safety of your arms
Surrounding me throughout each storm
And when the bitter winter wind
Would bid my very spirit bend
Your breath will keep me warm

Forgive me Lord, this fragile heart
Sometimes desires too much
Forgetting You are all I need
Then comes my tears, my plead
To stop and feel Your touch

I then can hear your gentle laugh

The love within Your voice

"My child I love you evermore

My gifts on you I freely pour

The best for you my choice"

Oh, Lord I want to stay right here

And sit here at Your feet

To never step away from You

And then I cannot lose my view

No chance for fear, defeat

"But child I ask then who would go

To tell the wounded broken heart

That I their lonely heart would mend

If not but you, who can I send?

If you refuse to start"

Then Father, Dear, I must say yes
To go and run Your bidding do
And You will cast aside my fears
Your hand will wipe away my tears
And keep my eyes on You

I know that You go with me now
You're ever present in my heart
I feel Your joy arise within
I feel Your wondrous strength again
Your love will ne'er depart

Effie Darlene Barba

BIBLIOGRAPHY

Bibi, Asia and Anne-Isabelle Tollet. *Blasphemy:A Memoir.* Chicago, IL: Chicago Press Review, 2013.

Bonhoeffer, Dietrich (trans. R.H. Fuller). *The Cost of Discipleship.* New York: Touchstone, 1955.

Edwards, Jonathan. "A Divine and Supernatural Light, immediately imparted to the Soul by the Spirit of God, shown to be both a Scriptural and Rational Doctrine-in a Sermon." *Digital Commons @ University of Nebraska-Lincoln.* n.d. http://digitalcommons.unl.edu/cgi/viewcontent.cgi?article=1056&context=etas (accessed October 28, 2017).

—. "Sinners in the Hands of an Angry God." *jonathan-edwards.org.* n.d. http://www.jonathan-edwards.org/Sinners.pdf (accessed October 21, 2017).

Emerson, Ralph Walso. *Ralph Waldo Emerson Quotes.* n.d. https://www.goodreads.com/quotes/416934-sow-a-thought-and=you-reap-an-action-sow-an (accessed October 22, 2017).

Featherstone, William R. "My Jesus I Love Thee, I Know Thou Art Mine (1864)." *Hymnary.org.* n.d. https://hymnary.org/text/my_jesus_i_love_thee_i _know_thou_art_mi (accessed October 22, 2017).

Giglio, Louis. *i am not; but I know I AM.* Sisters, OR: Multinomah Publishers, 2005.

Hamilton, Robert Browning. "quotes by Robert Browning Hamilton." *Goodreads.com.* n.d. https://www.goodreads.com/quotes/289683-i-walked-a-mile-with-pleasure-she-chatted-all-the (accessed October 24, 2017).

Lewis, C.S. *Mere Christianity.* New York: Macmillan, 1952.

Newton, John and Richard Cecil. *Memoirs of the Rev. John Newton in The Works of the Re. John Newton, Vol.1.* Edinburgh: The Banner of Truth Trust, 1985.

Richardson, Bobby. "Prayer at Fellowship of Christian Athletes." *pastorterryblog.wordpress.com.* 02 28, 1010. https://pastorterryblog.wordpress.com/2010/02/ 28/sunday-sermon-your-will-nothing-more-nothing-less-nothing-else (accessed October 21, 2017).

Sartre, Jean Paul. *Nausea.* New York: New Directions, 1964, 1964.

Sartre, Jean Paul, and trans. H. Barnes. *Being and Nothingness.* New York: Washington Square Press, 1969.

Spurgeon, C.H. *Christ's Glorious Achievements.* Great Britain: Christian Focus, n.d.

Stanley, Charles. "God's Children Gifted for Ministry."
     InTouch.org. 2010. https://store.intouch.org/p-
     2654-gods-children-gifted-for-ministry.aspx
     (accessed October 26, 2017).

—. "Life Principle 2: A Life of Obedience." *Intouch.org.* July
     2, 2014. https://www.intouch.org/read/life-
     principle-2-a-life-of-obedience (accessed October 2,
     2017).

Strong, James. *Strong's Exhaustive Concordance.* Peabody,
     MA: Hendrickson's, 2007.

Thoreau, Henry David. *Walden.* New York: Thomas Y
     Crowell, 1910.

Zodhiates, Spiro. *Complete World Study Dictionary: New
     Testament.* Chattanooga, TN: AMG Publishers,
     1993.

Matt
918 694-4055
Angela 918-693-6036

80371178R00188

Made in the USA
Columbia, SC
16 November 2017